GRAPHIC HISTORY

# THE BOSTON TEA PARTY

by Matt Doeden

illustrated by Charles Barnett III
and Dave Hoover

Consultant
Nancy M. Godleski
Kaplanoff Librarian for American History
Sterling Memorial Library, Yale University
New Haven, Connecticut

Capstone press

Mankato, Minnesota

Graphic Library is published by Capstone Press,
1710 Roe Crest Drive, North Mankato, Minnesota 56003.
www.capstonepub.com

Books published by Capstone Press are manufactured with paper
containing at least 10 percent post-consumer waste.

*Library of Congress Cataloging-in-Publication Data*
Doeden, Matt.
    The Boston Tea Party / by Matt Doeden; illustrated by Charles Barnett III and Dave Hoover.
    p. cm.— (Graphic library. Graphic history.)
    Includes bibliographical references and index.
    ISBN-13: 978-0-7368-3846-7 (hardcover)        ISBN-10: 0-7368-3846-5 (hardcover)
    ISBN-13: 978-0-7368-5243-2 (softcover pbk.)    ISBN-10: 0-7368-5243-3 (softcover pbk.)
1. Boston Tea Party, 1773—Juvenile literature. I. Barnett, Charles, III ill. II. Title. III. Series.
E215.7.D64 2005
973.3'115—dc22                                                        2004015500

Summary: Describes the events of the Boston Tea Party, one of the acts by American Patriots that
    led to the American Revolution.

**Editor's note:** Direct quotations from primary sources are indicated by a yellow background.

Direct quotations appear on the following pages:
Page 9, from *John Adams: A Life* by John Ferling (University of Tennessee Press, 1992).
Pages 12, 22, from *Samuel Adams* by James K. Hosmer (New York: Houghton Mifflin Company,
    1898).
Page 23, from *The Writings of Samuel Adams* edited by Harry Alonzo Cushing. (New York:
    Octagon Books, 1968).

**Credits**

**Art Directors**
Jason Knudson, Heather Kindseth

**Storyboard Artist**
Dave Hoover

**Editor**
Erika L. Shores

**Acknowledgments**
Capstone Press thanks Philip Charles
Crawford, Library Director, Essex High
School, Essex, Vermont, and columnist
for *Knowledge Quest*, for his assistance
in the preparation of this book.

Capstone Press thanks Charles Barnett III
and Dave Hoover of Cavalier Graphics.

Printed in the United States of America in North Mankato, Minnesota.
042018    000022

# TABLE OF CONTENTS

# Chapter 1
# A Tax on Tea

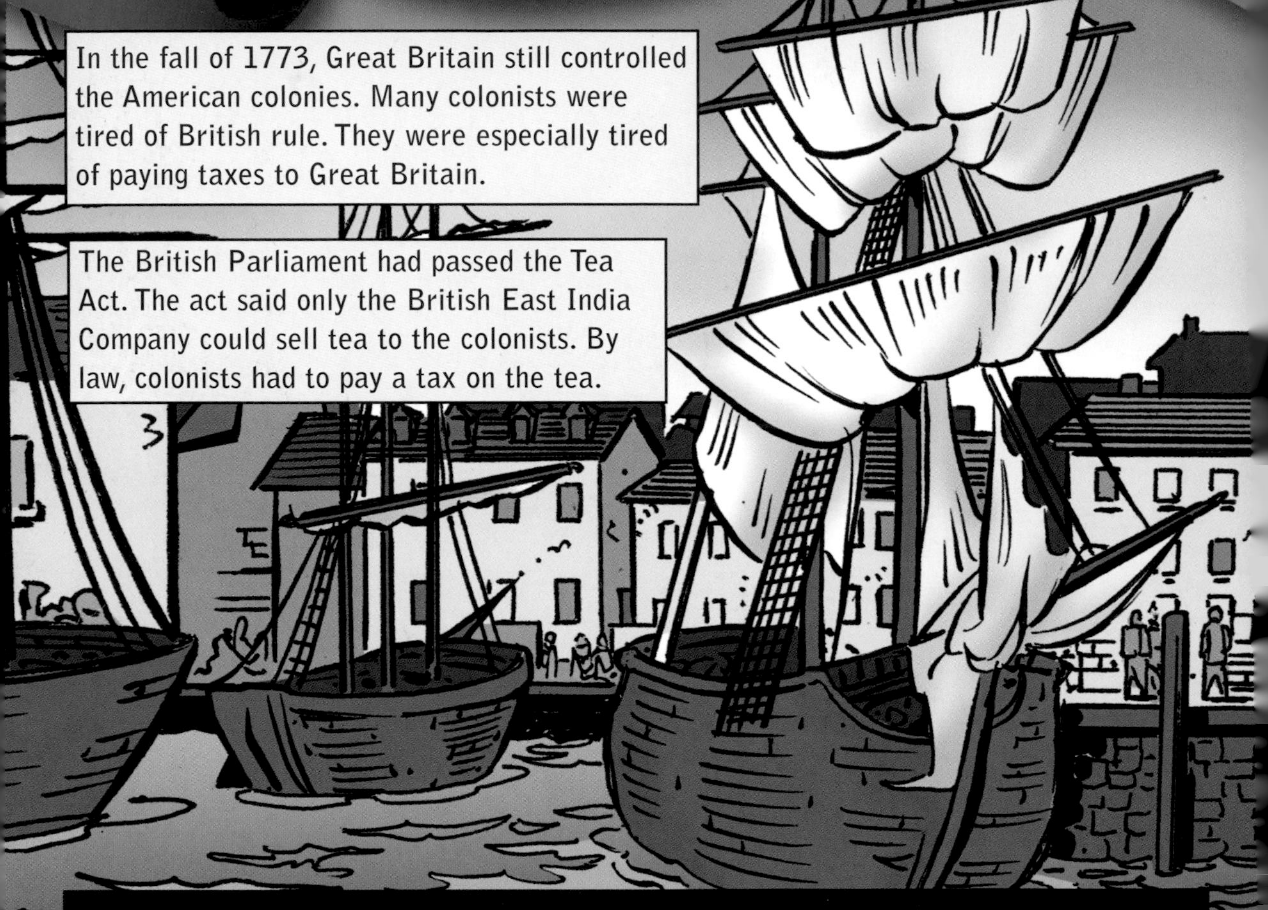
In the fall of 1773, Great Britain still controlled the American colonies. Many colonists were tired of British rule. They were especially tired of paying taxes to Great Britain.
The British Parliament had passed the Tea Act. The act said only the British East India Company could sell tea to the colonists. By law, colonists had to pay a tax on the tea.

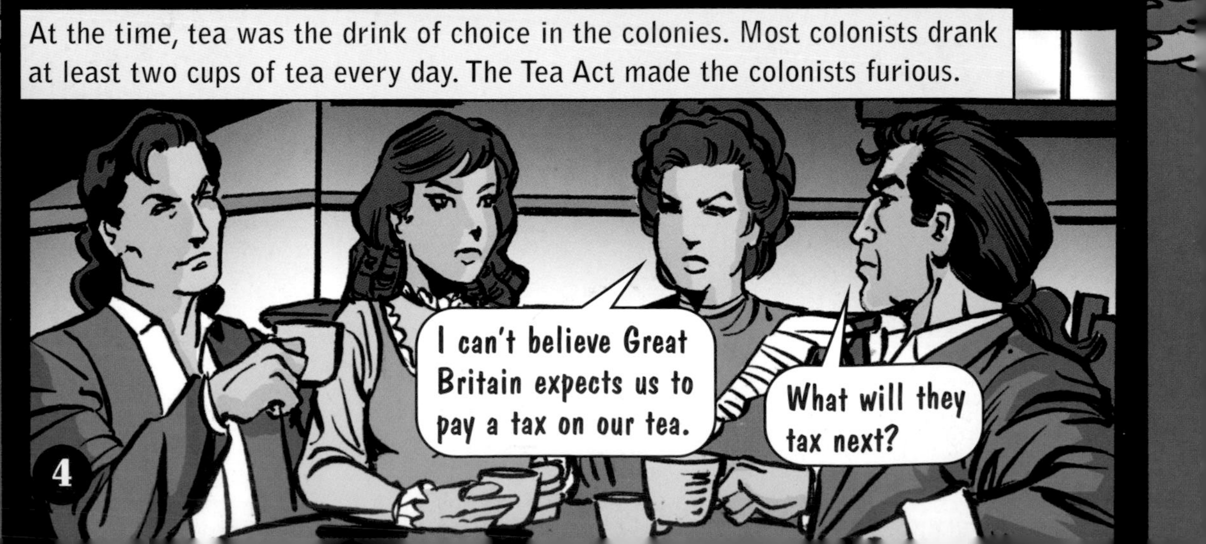
At the time, tea was the drink of choice in the colonies. Most colonists drank at least two cups of tea every day. The Tea Act made the colonists furious.
I can't believe Great Britain expects us to pay a tax on our tea.
What will they tax next?

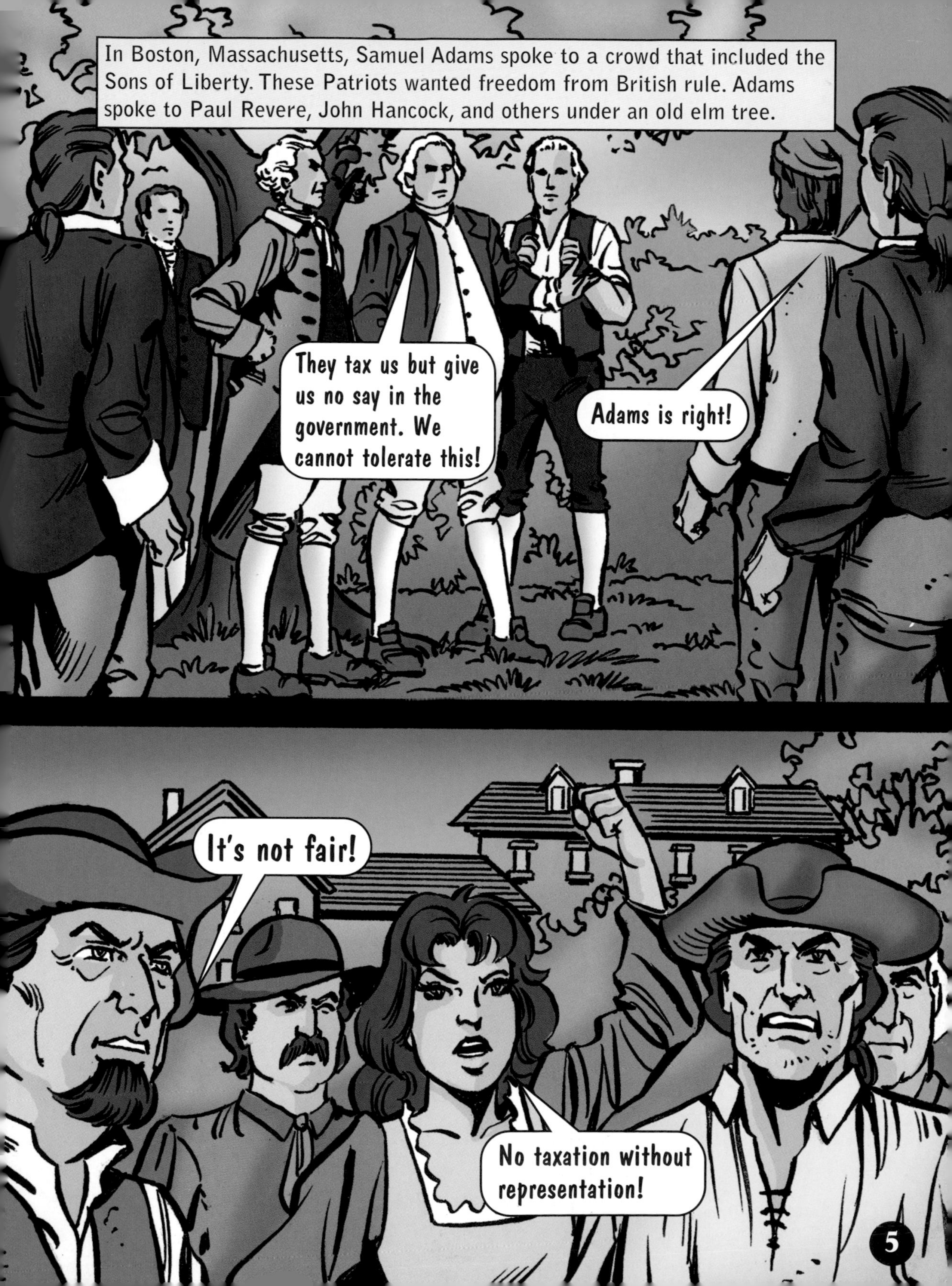
In Boston, Massachusetts, Samuel Adams spoke to a crowd that included the Sons of Liberty. These Patriots wanted freedom from British rule. Adams spoke to Paul Revere, John Hancock, and others under an old elm tree.
They tax us but give us no say in the government. We cannot tolerate this!
Adams is right!
It's not fair!
No taxation without representation!

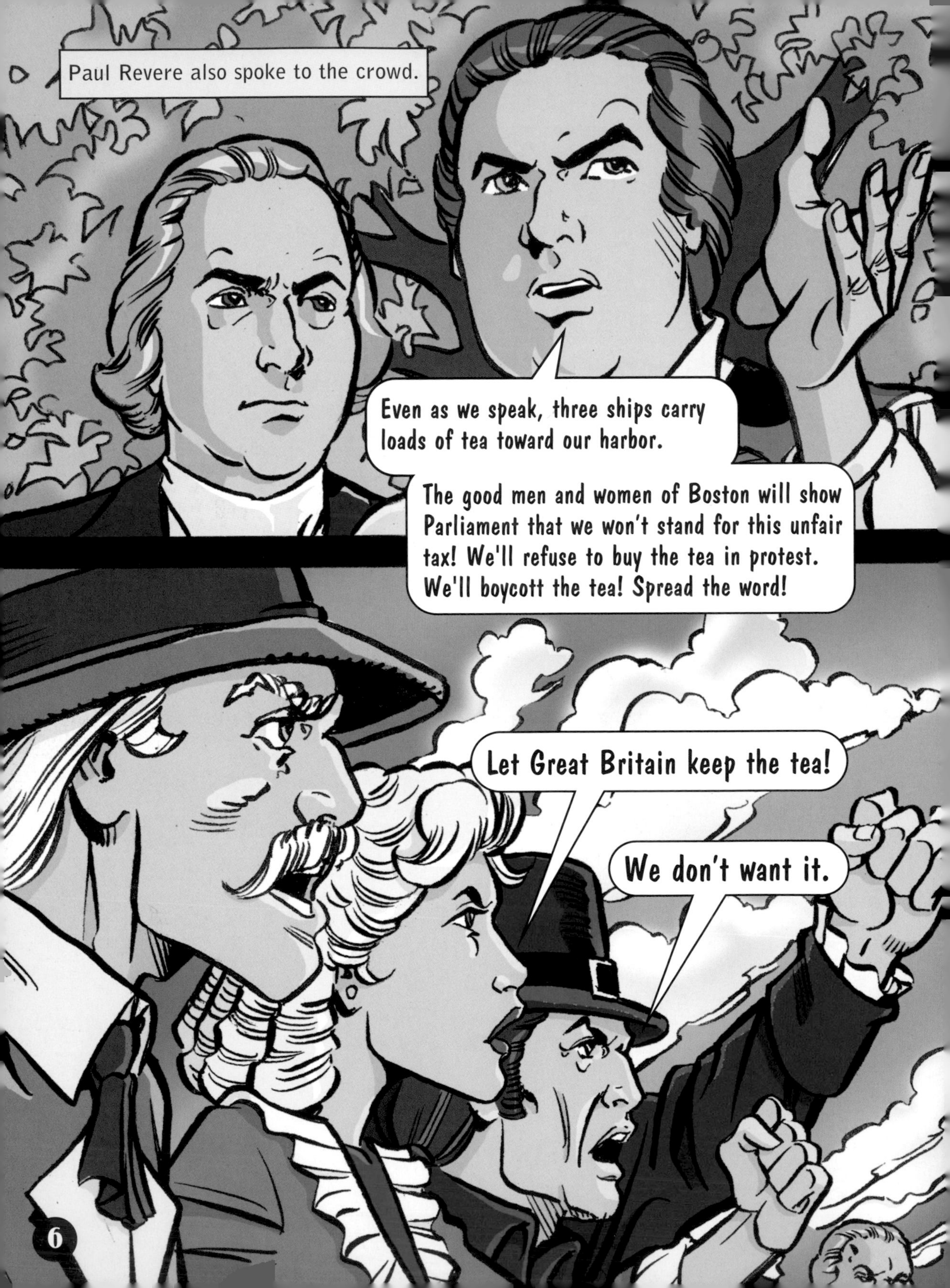
Paul Revere also spoke to the crowd.
Even as we speak, three ships carry loads of tea toward our harbor.
The good men and women of Boston will show Parliament that we won't stand for this unfair tax! We'll refuse to buy the tea in protest. We'll boycott the tea! Spread the word!
Let Great Britain keep the tea!
We don't want it.

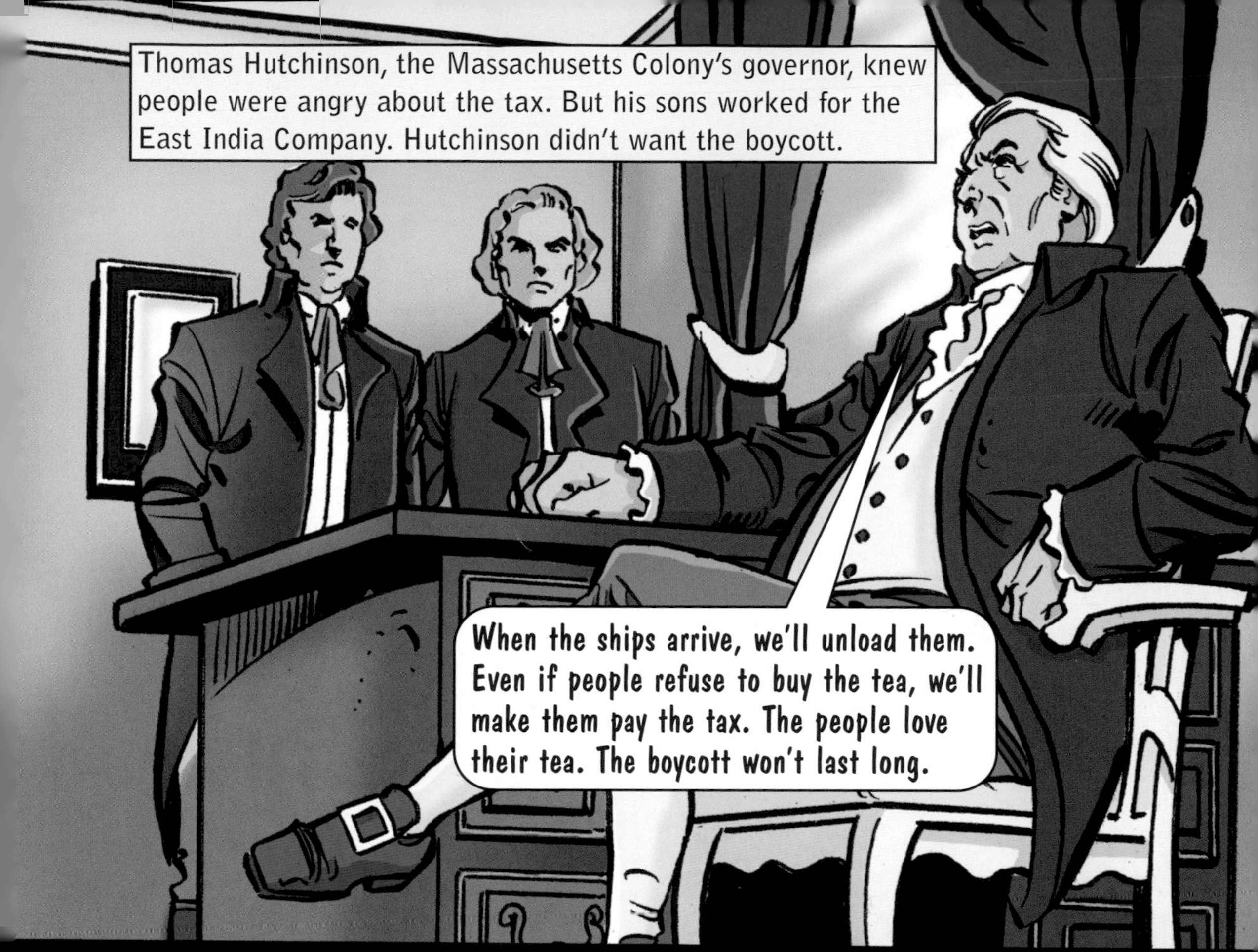
Thomas Hutchinson, the Massachusetts Colony's governor, knew people were angry about the tax. But his sons worked for the East India Company. Hutchinson didn't want the boycott.
When the ships arrive, we'll unload them. Even if people refuse to buy the tea, we'll make them pay the tax. The people love their tea. The boycott won't last long.

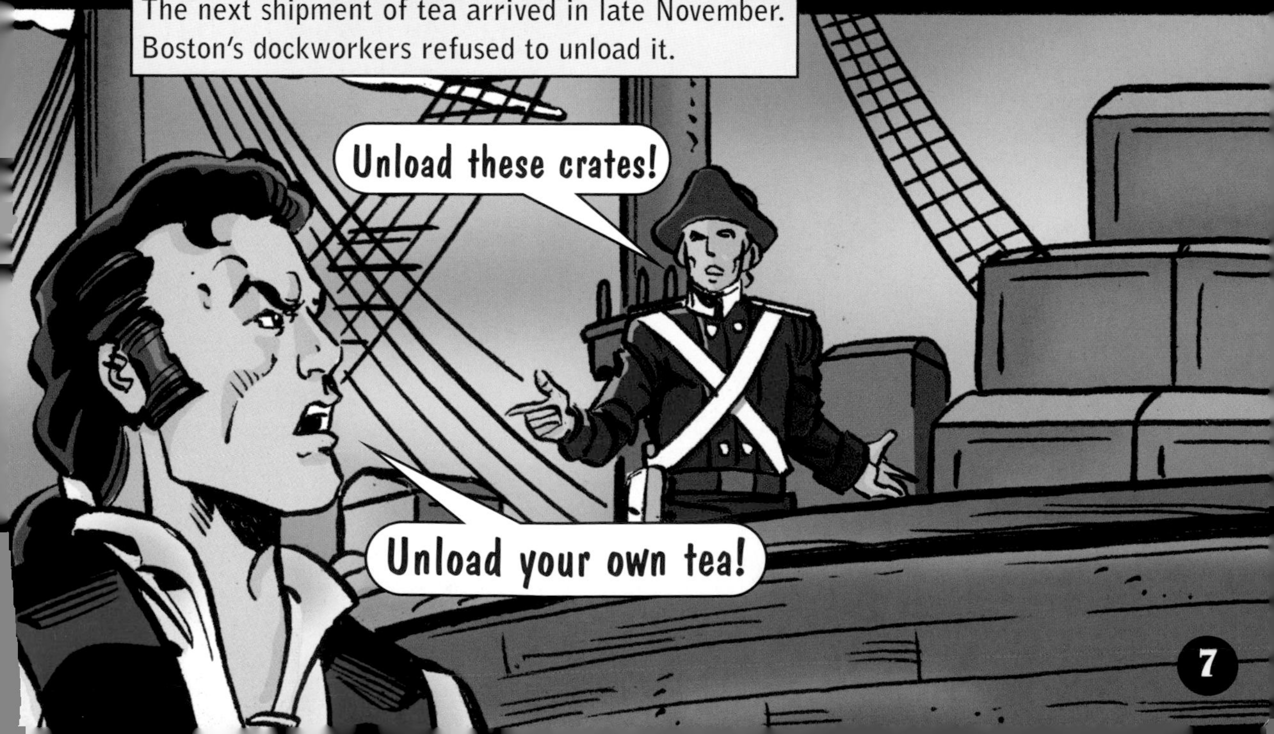
The next shipment of tea arrived in late November. Boston's dockworkers refused to unload it.
Unload these crates!
Unload your own tea!

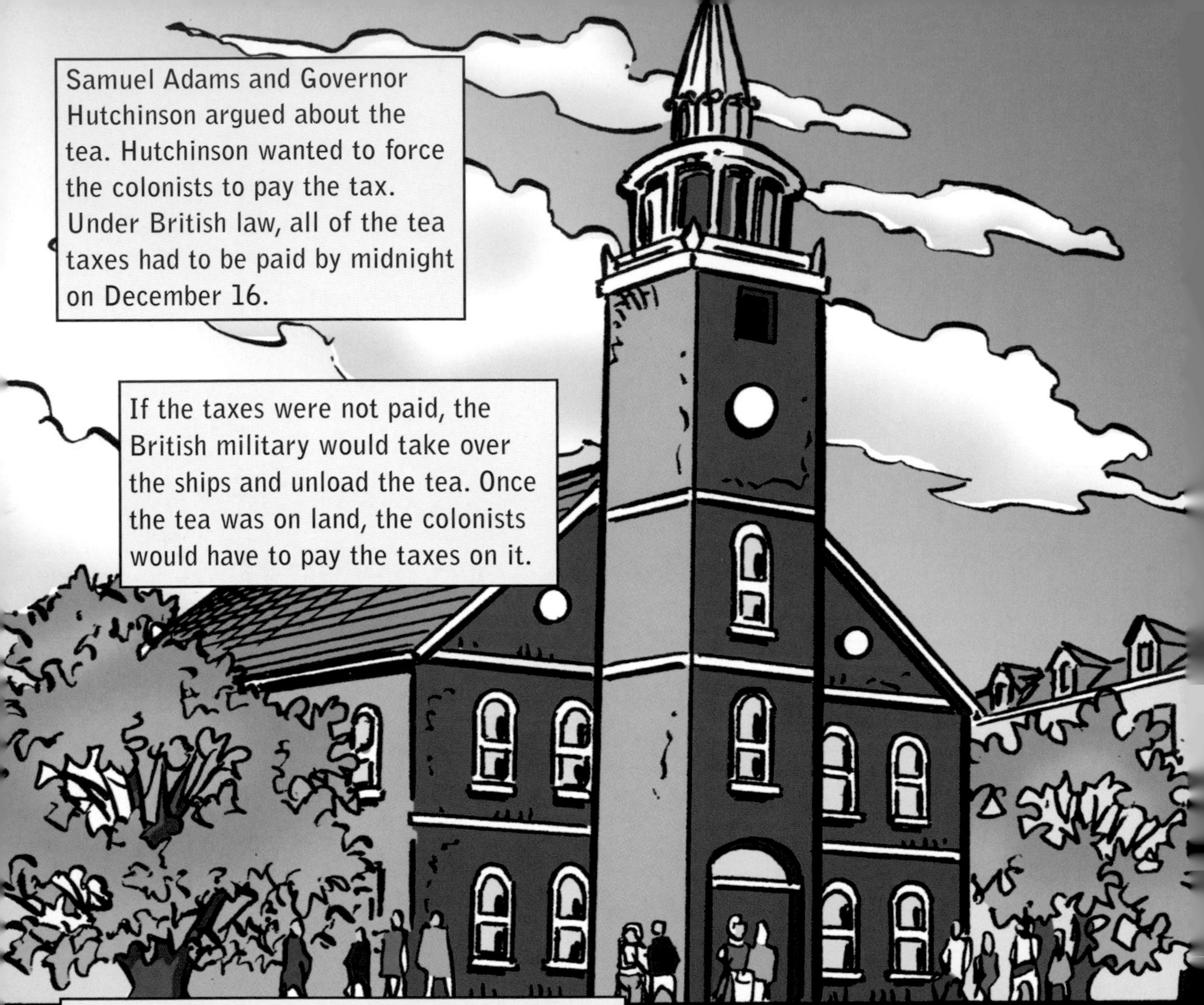
Samuel Adams and Governor Hutchinson argued about the tea. Hutchinson wanted to force the colonists to pay the tax. Under British law, all of the tea taxes had to be paid by midnight on December 16.
If the taxes were not paid, the British military would take over the ships and unload the tea. Once the tea was on land, the colonists would have to pay the taxes on it.

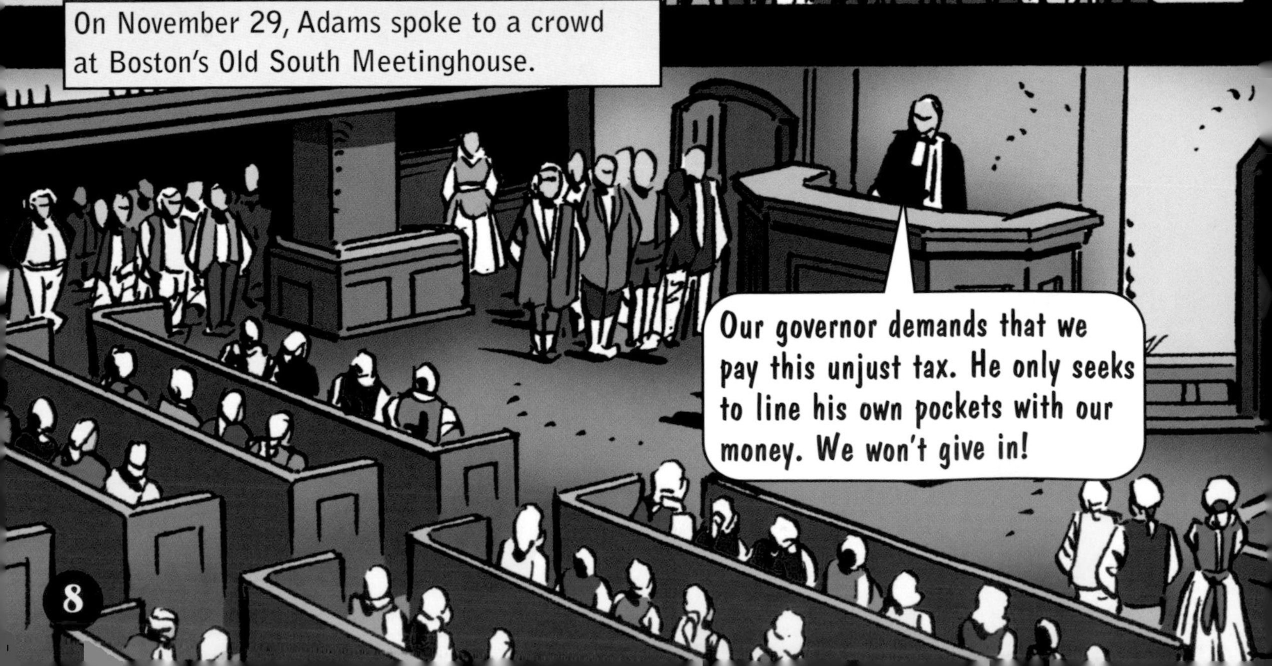
On November 29, Adams spoke to a crowd at Boston's Old South Meetinghouse.
Our governor demands that we pay this unjust tax. He only seeks to line his own pockets with our money. We won't give in!

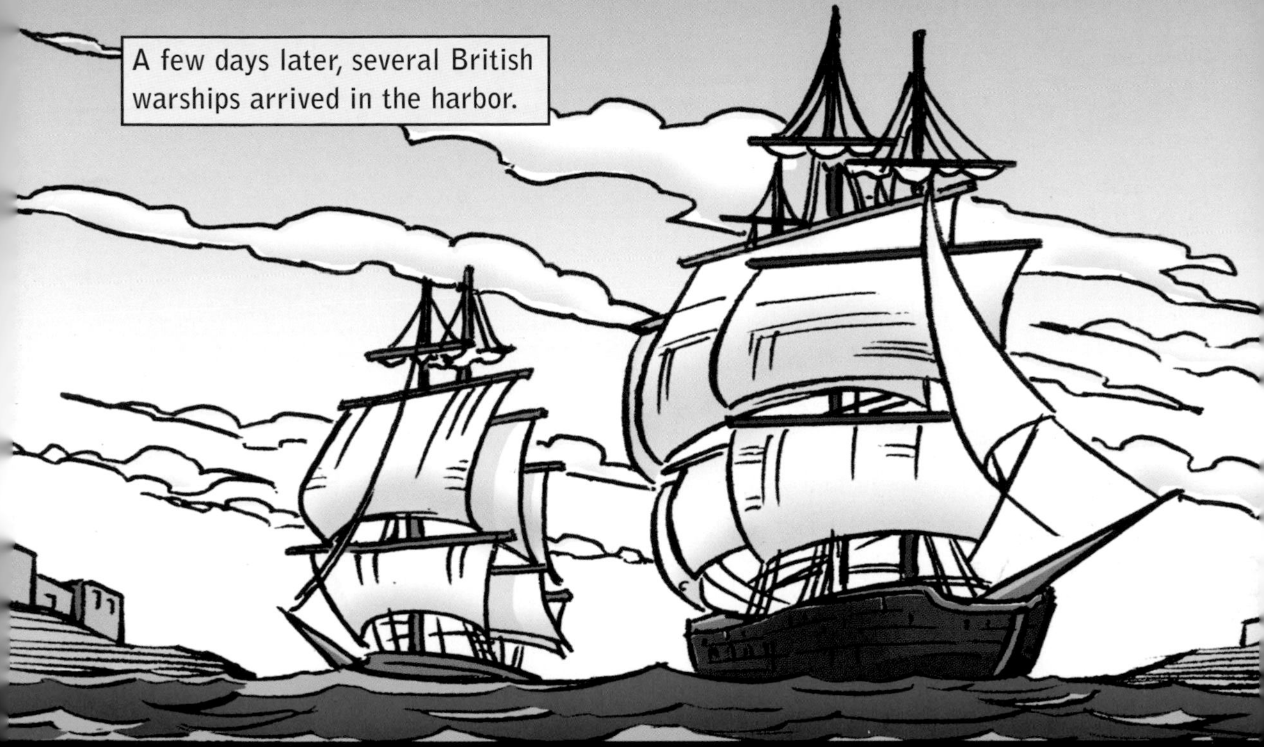
A few days later, several British warships arrived in the harbor.

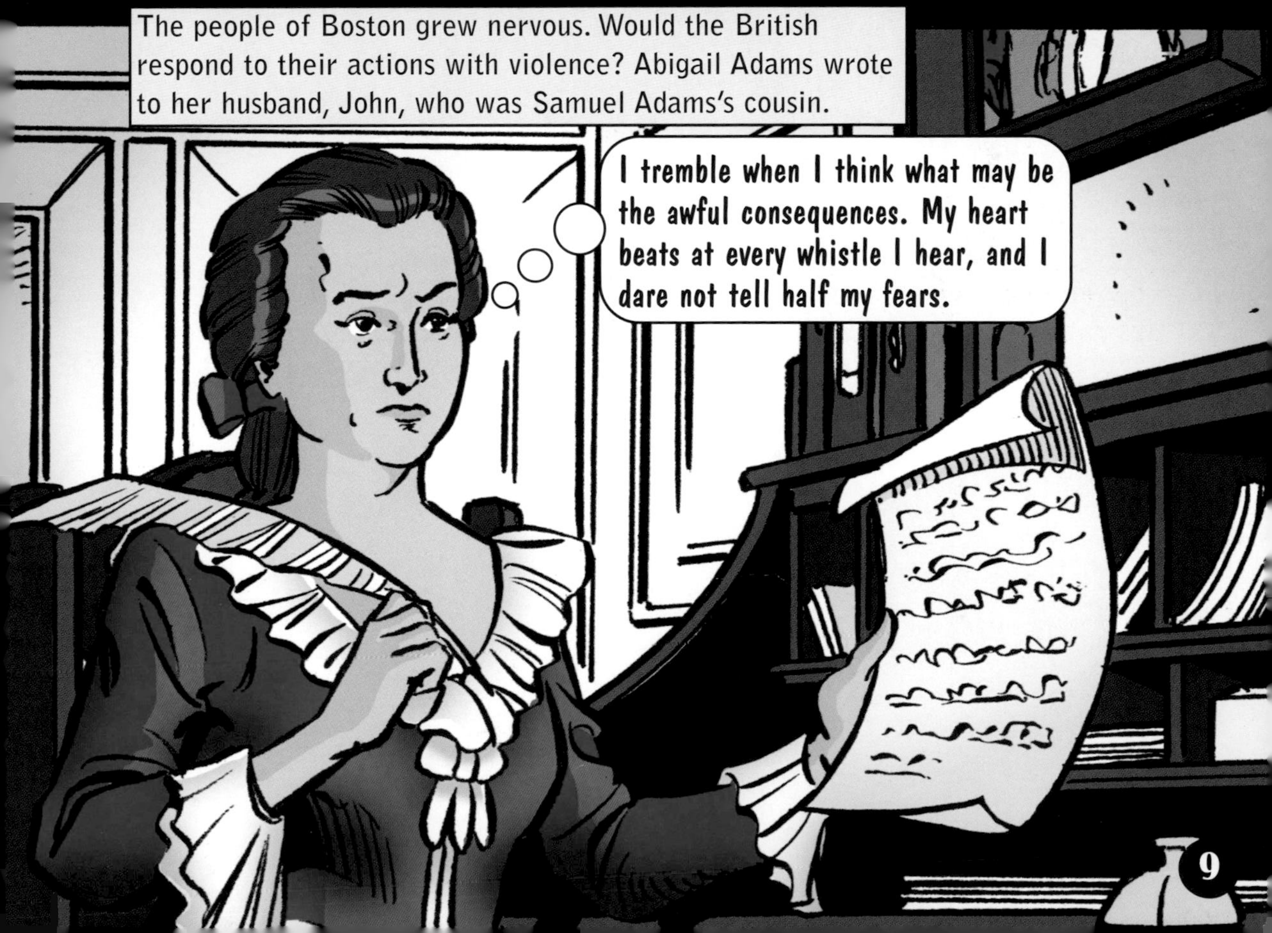
The people of Boston grew nervous. Would the British respond to their actions with violence? Abigail Adams wrote to her husband, John, who was Samuel Adams's cousin.
I tremble when I think what may be the awful consequences. My heart beats at every whistle I hear, and I dare not tell half my fears.

# CHAPTER 2 A DECISION MADE

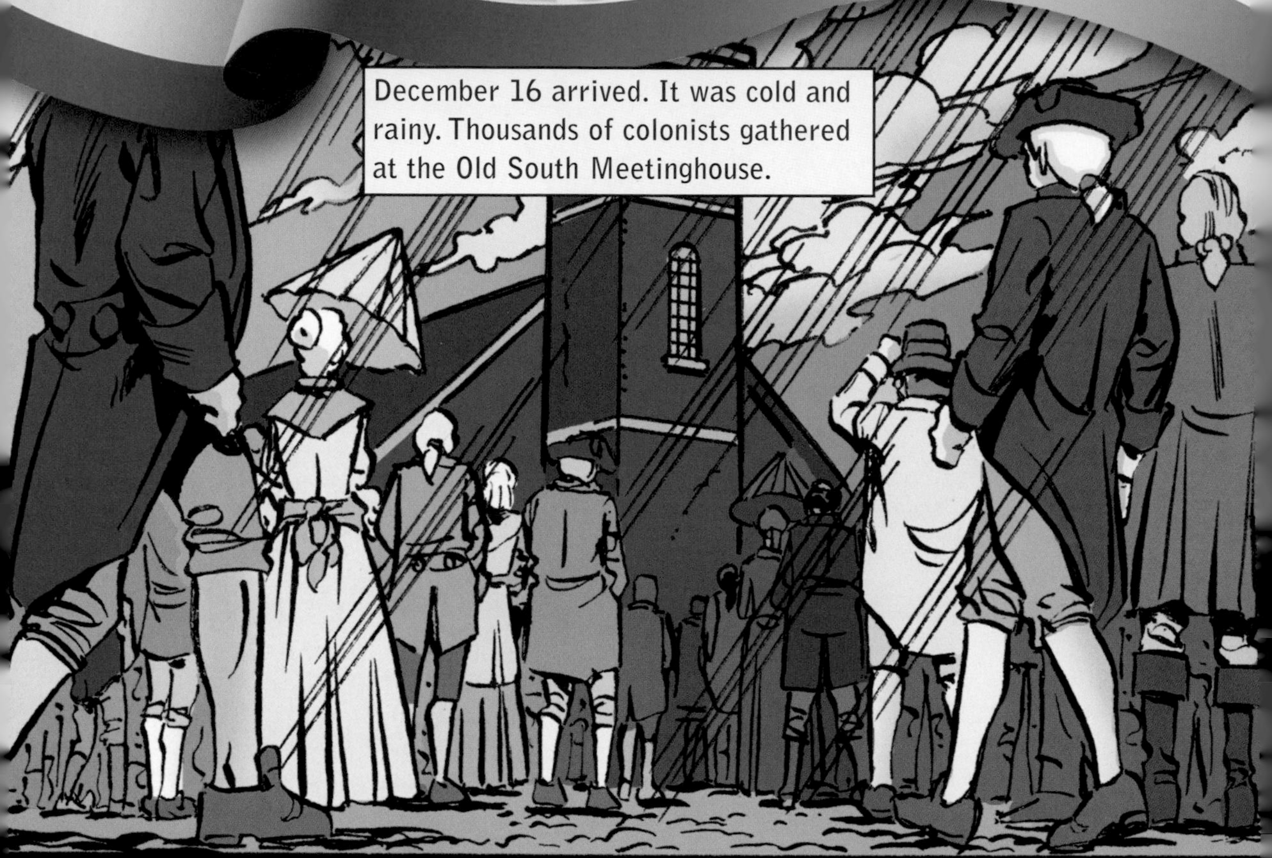
December 16 arrived. It was cold and rainy. Thousands of colonists gathered at the Old South Meetinghouse.

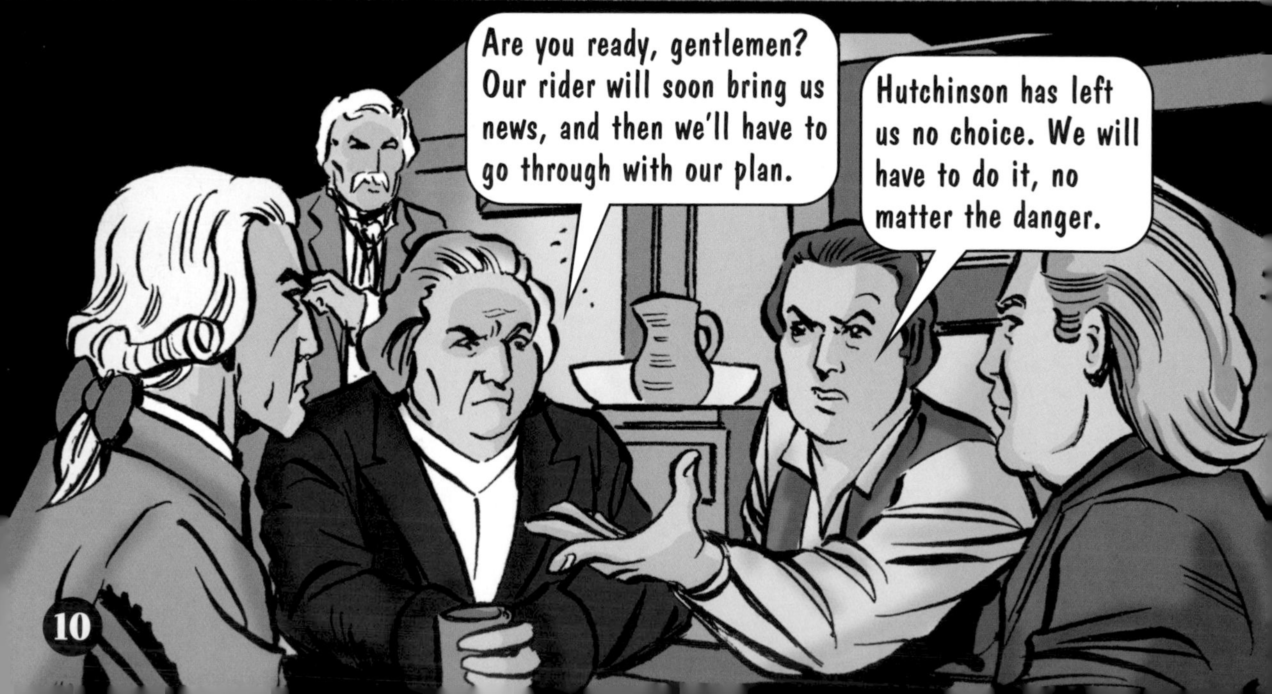
Are you ready, gentlemen? Our rider will soon bring us news, and then we'll have to go through with our plan.
Hutchinson has left us no choice. We will have to do it, no matter the danger.

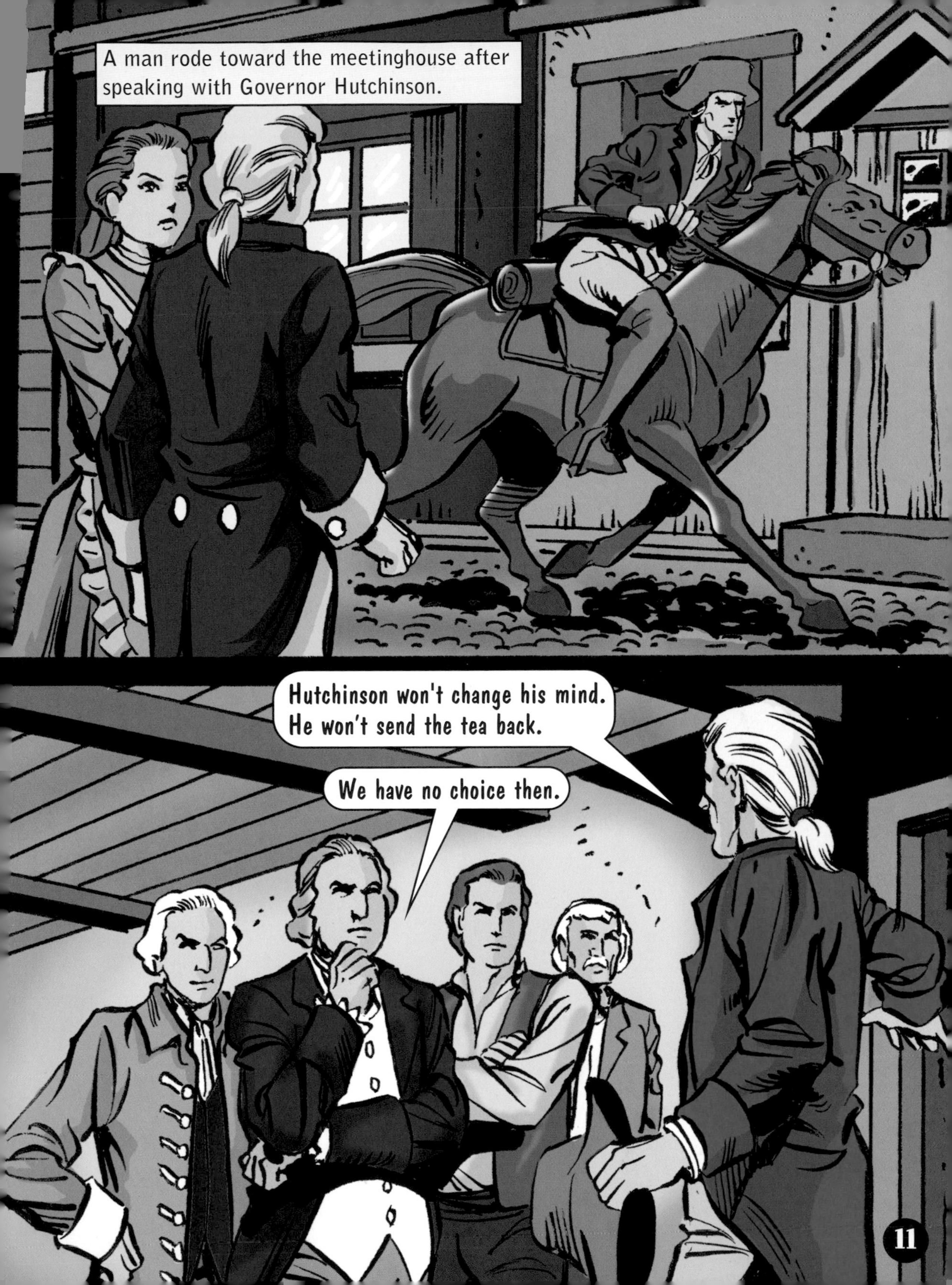
A man rode toward the meetinghouse after speaking with Governor Hutchinson.
Hutchinson won't change his mind. He won't send the tea back.
We have no choice then.

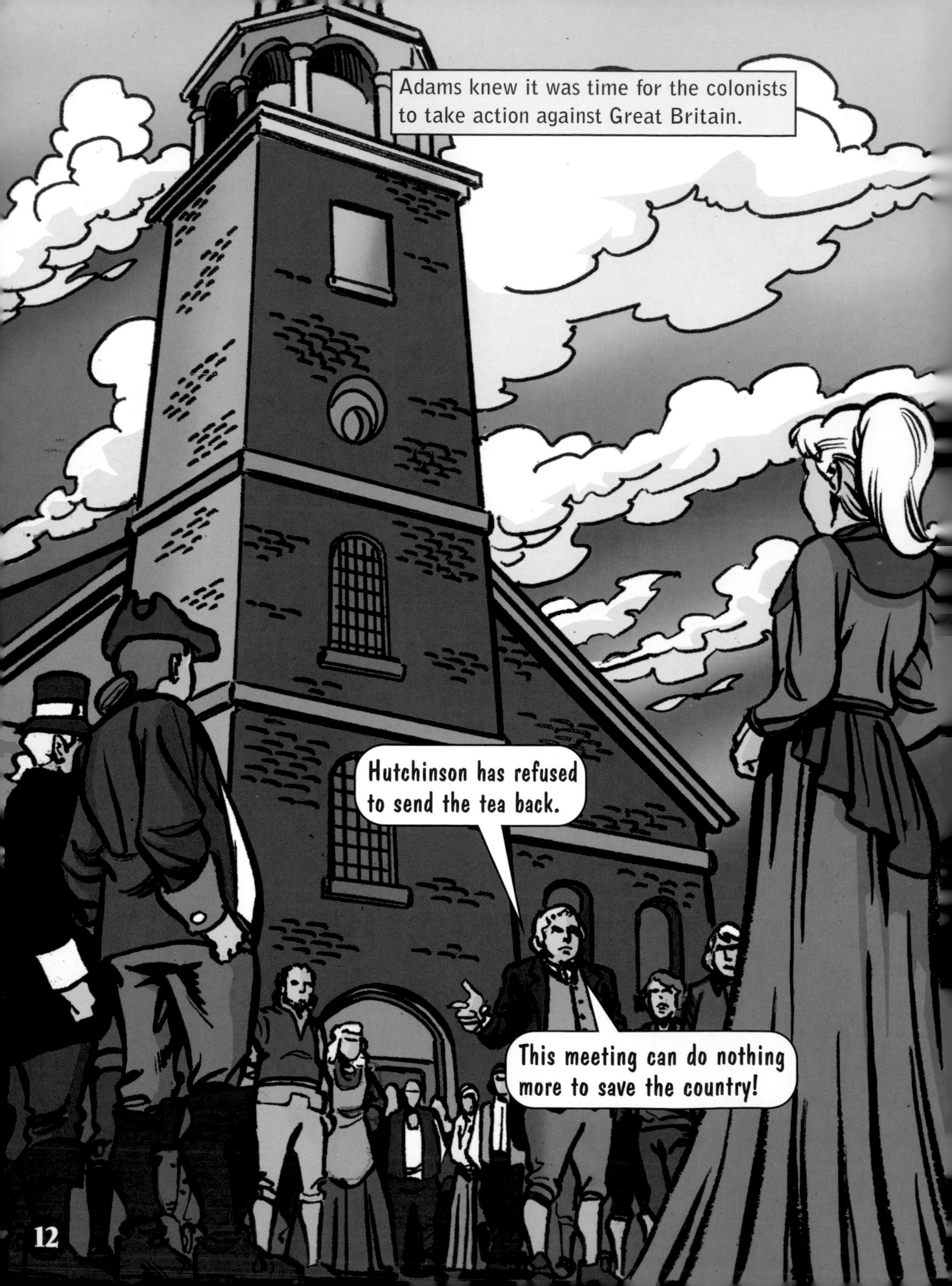
Adams knew it was time for the colonists to take action against Great Britain.
Hutchinson has refused to send the tea back.
This meeting can do nothing more to save the country!

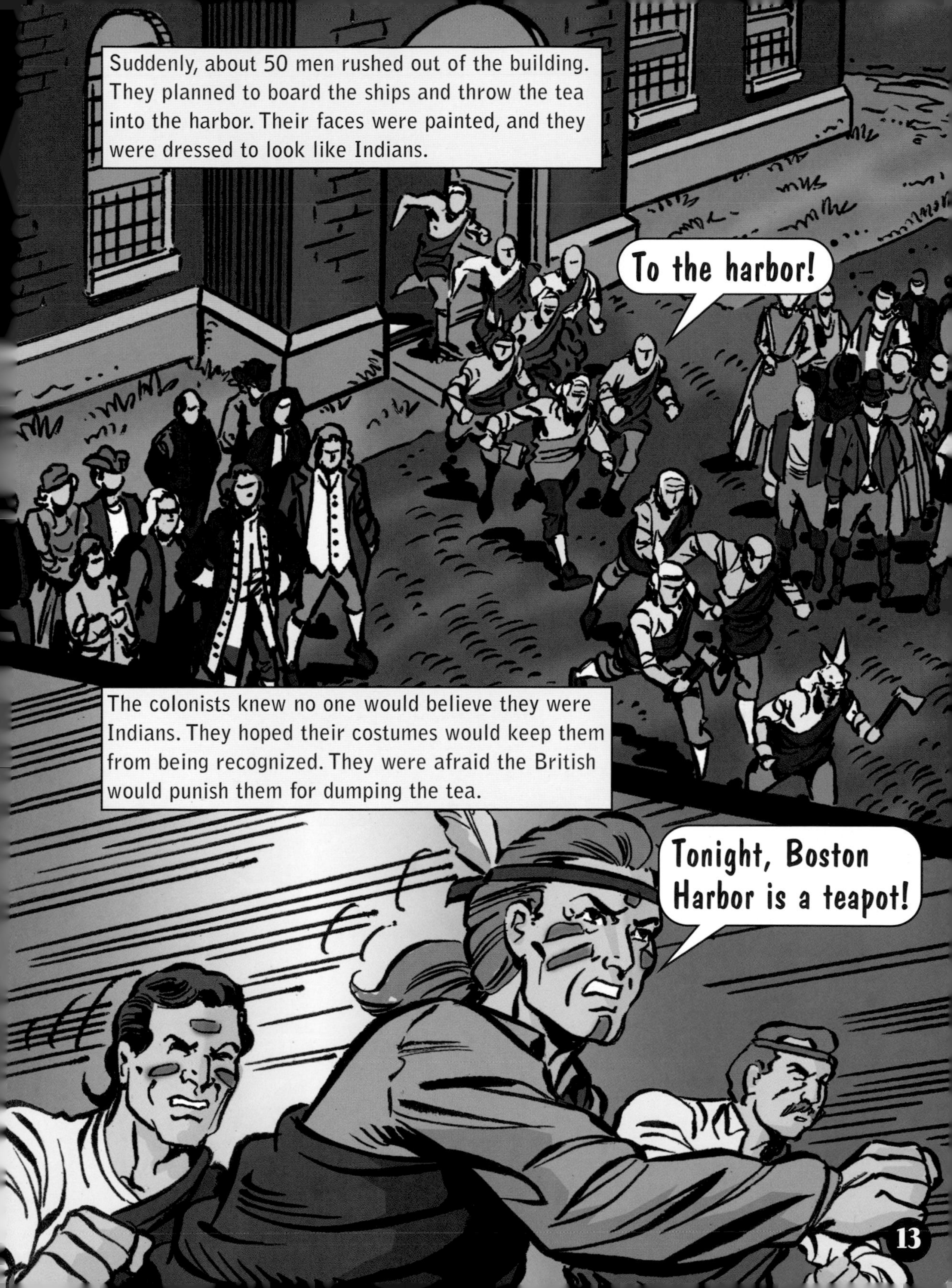
Suddenly, about 50 men rushed out of the building. They planned to board the ships and throw the tea into the harbor. Their faces were painted, and they were dressed to look like Indians.
To the harbor!
The colonists knew no one would believe they were Indians. They hoped their costumes would keep them from being recognized. They were afraid the British would punish them for dumping the tea.
Tonight, Boston Harbor is a teapot!

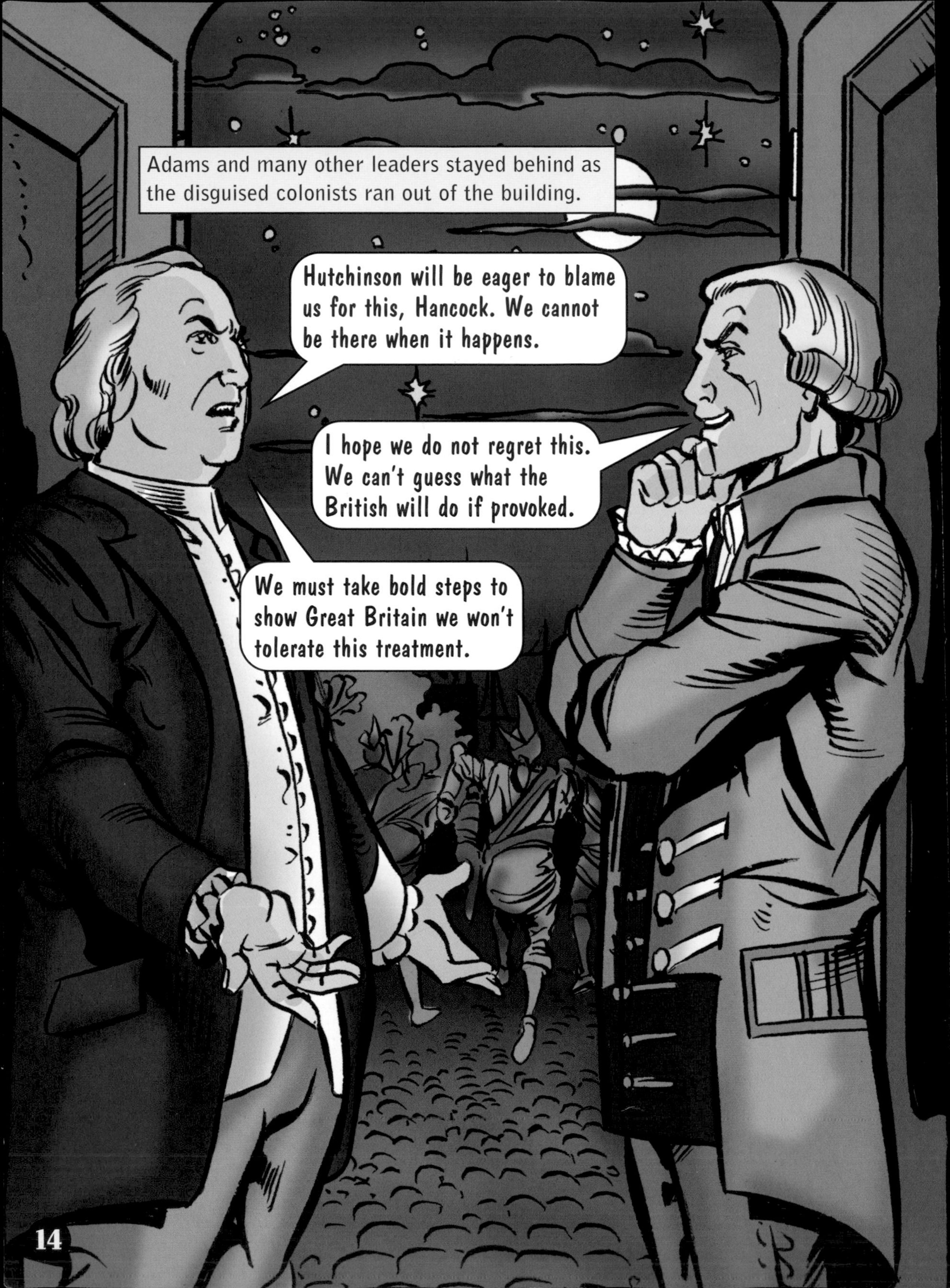
Adams and many other leaders stayed behind as the disguised colonists ran out of the building.
Hutchinson will be eager to blame us for this, Hancock. We cannot be there when it happens.
I hope we do not regret this. We can't guess what the British will do if provoked.
We must take bold steps to show Great Britain we won't tolerate this treatment.

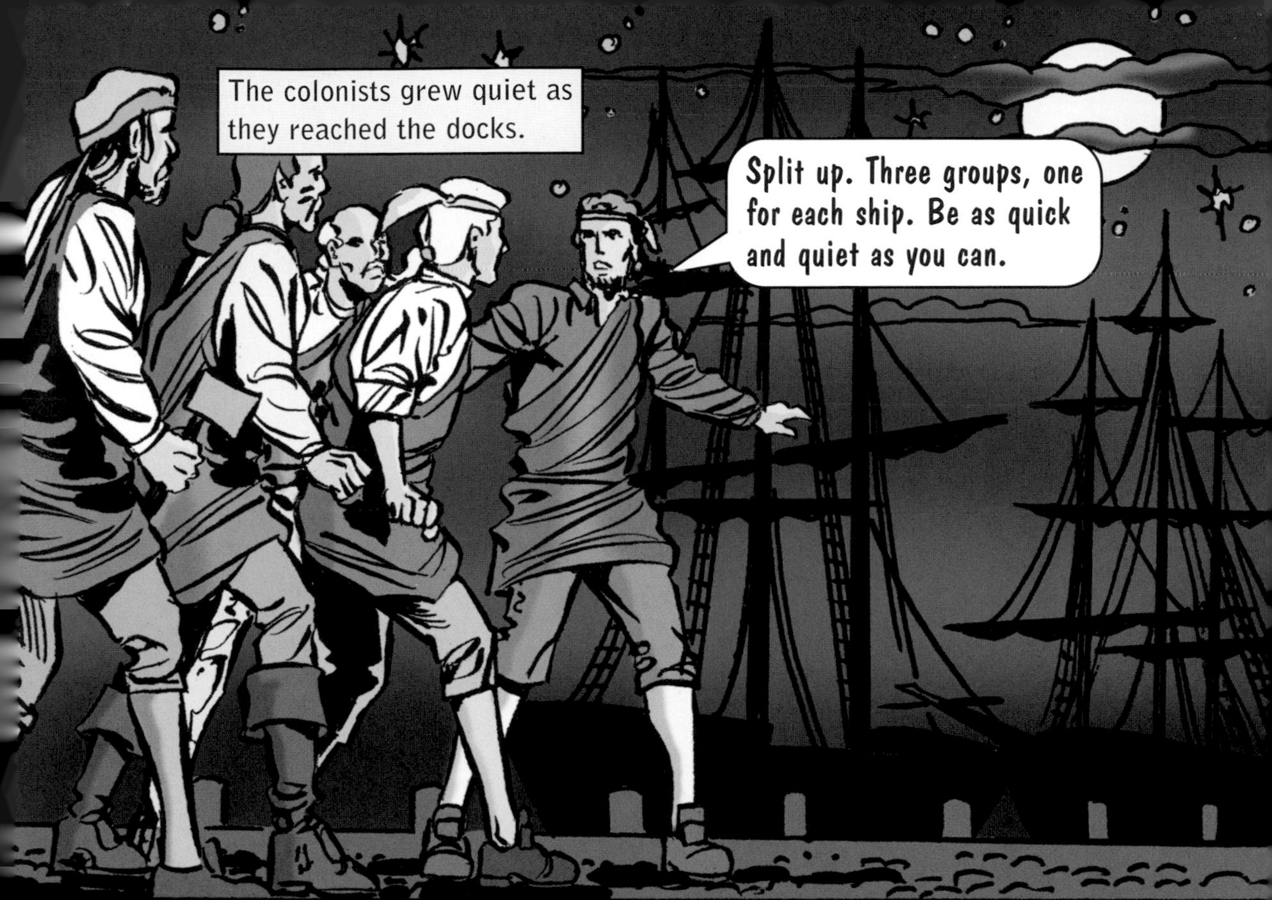
The colonists grew quiet as they reached the docks.
Split up. Three groups, one for each ship. Be as quick and quiet as you can.

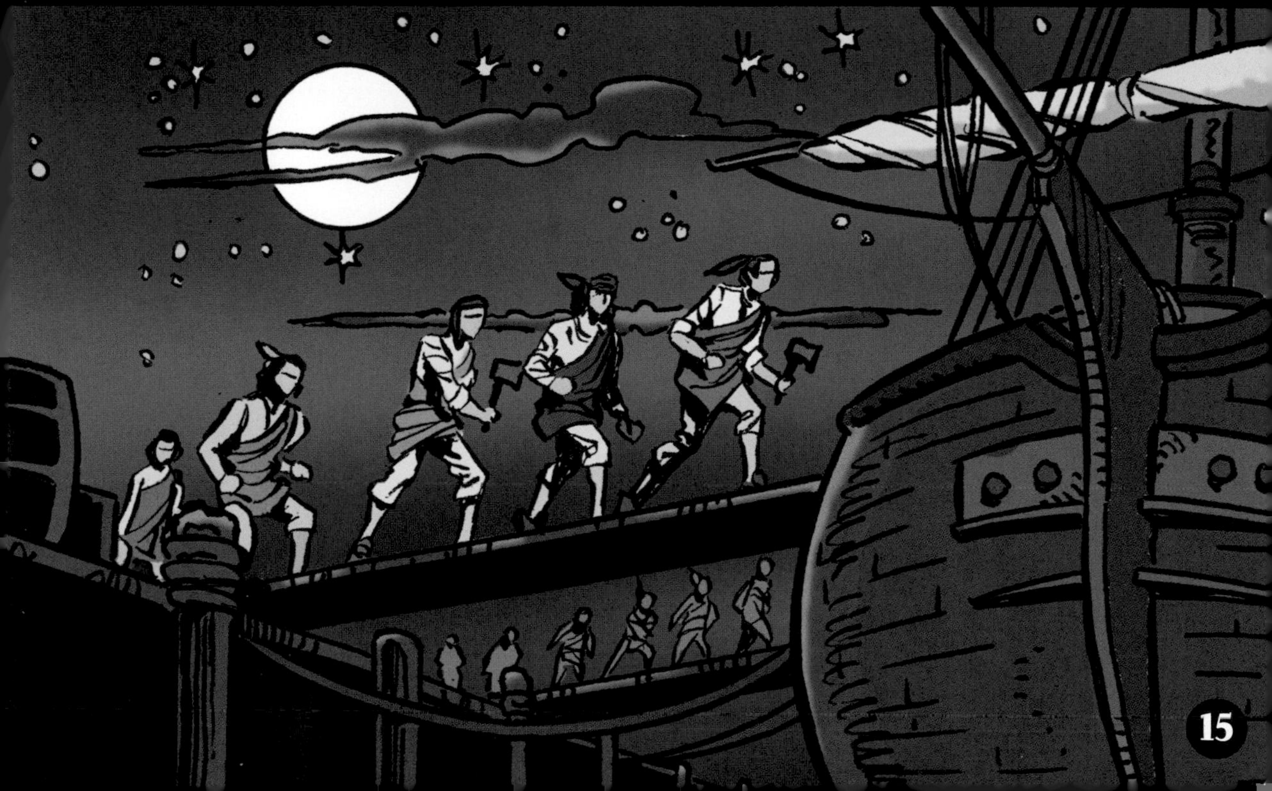

# Chapter 3 Destroying the Tea

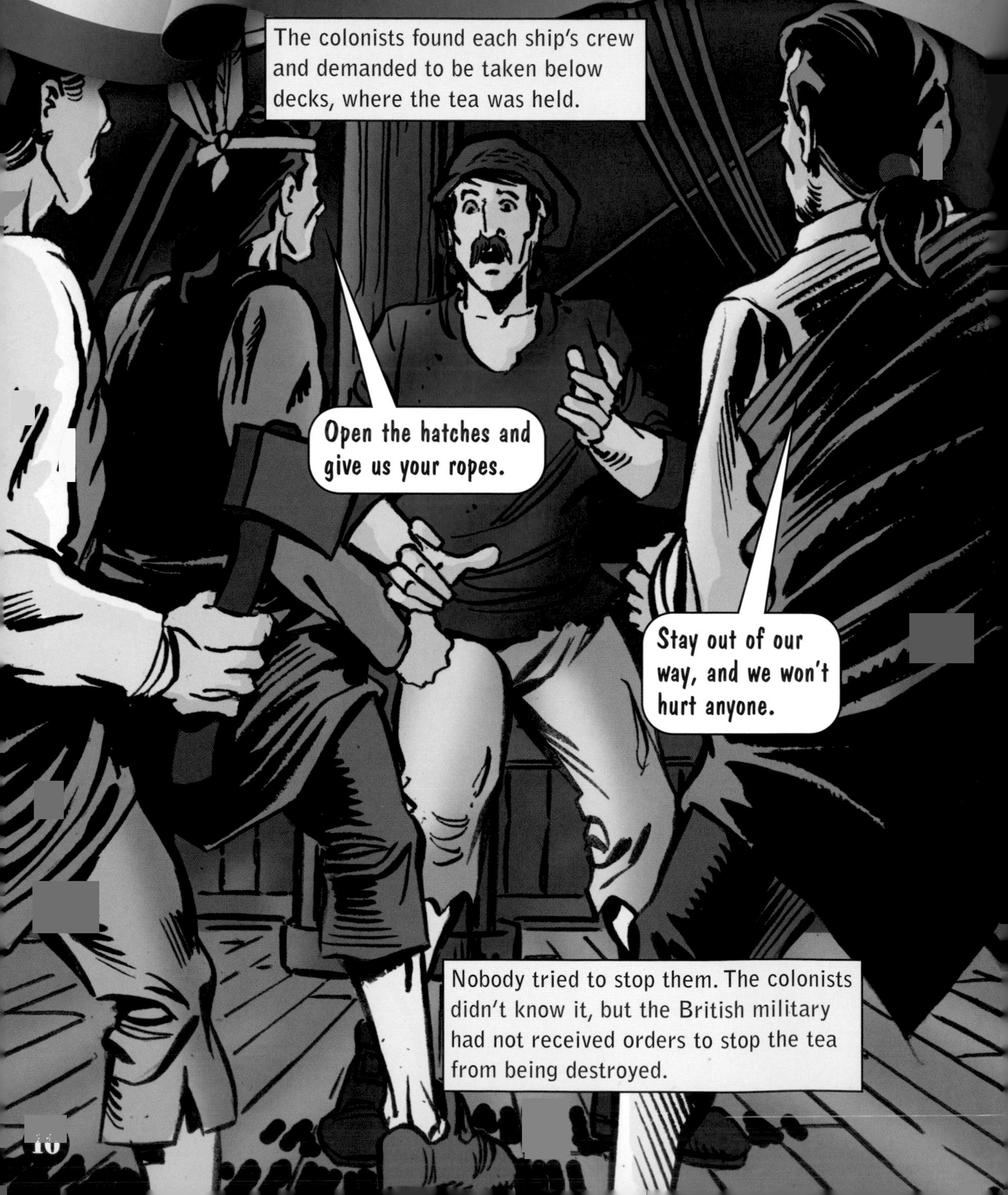
The colonists found each ship's crew and demanded to be taken below decks, where the tea was held.
Open the hatches and give us your ropes.
Stay out of our way, and we won't hurt anyone.
Nobody tried to stop them. The colonists didn't know it, but the British military had not received orders to stop the tea from being destroyed.

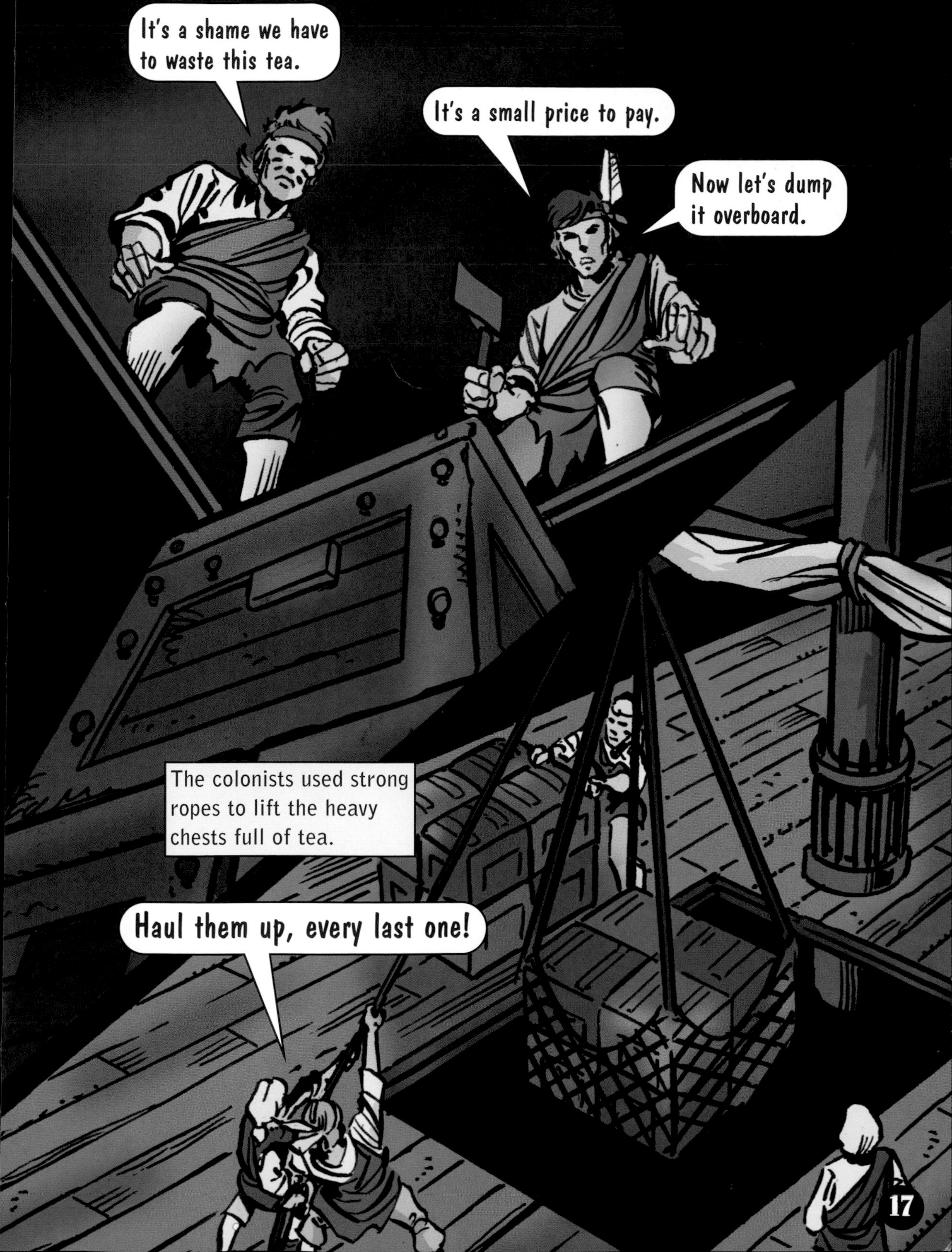
It's a shame we have to waste this tea.
It's a small price to pay.
Now let's dump it overboard.
The colonists used strong ropes to lift the heavy chests full of tea.
Haul them up, every last one!

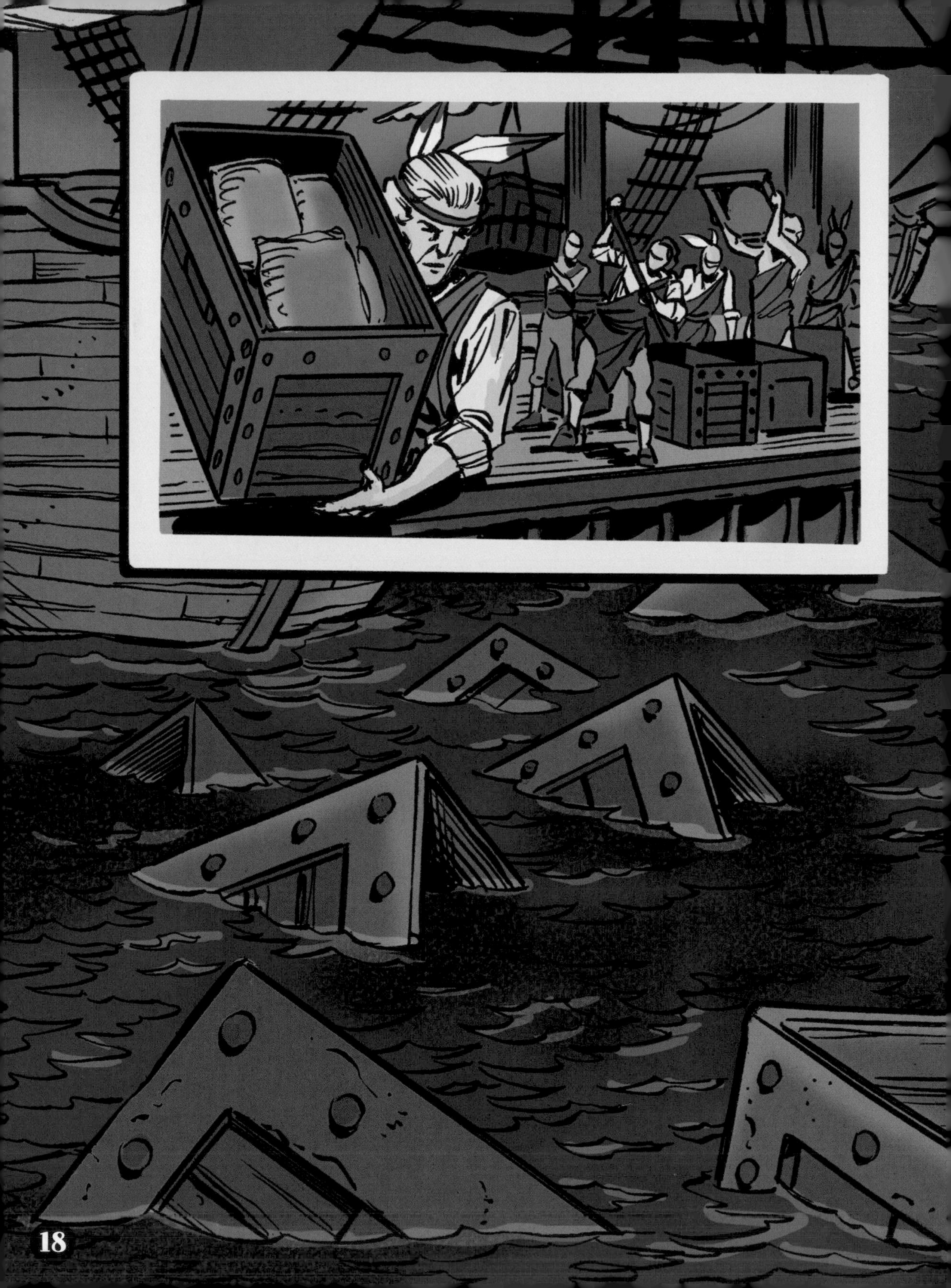

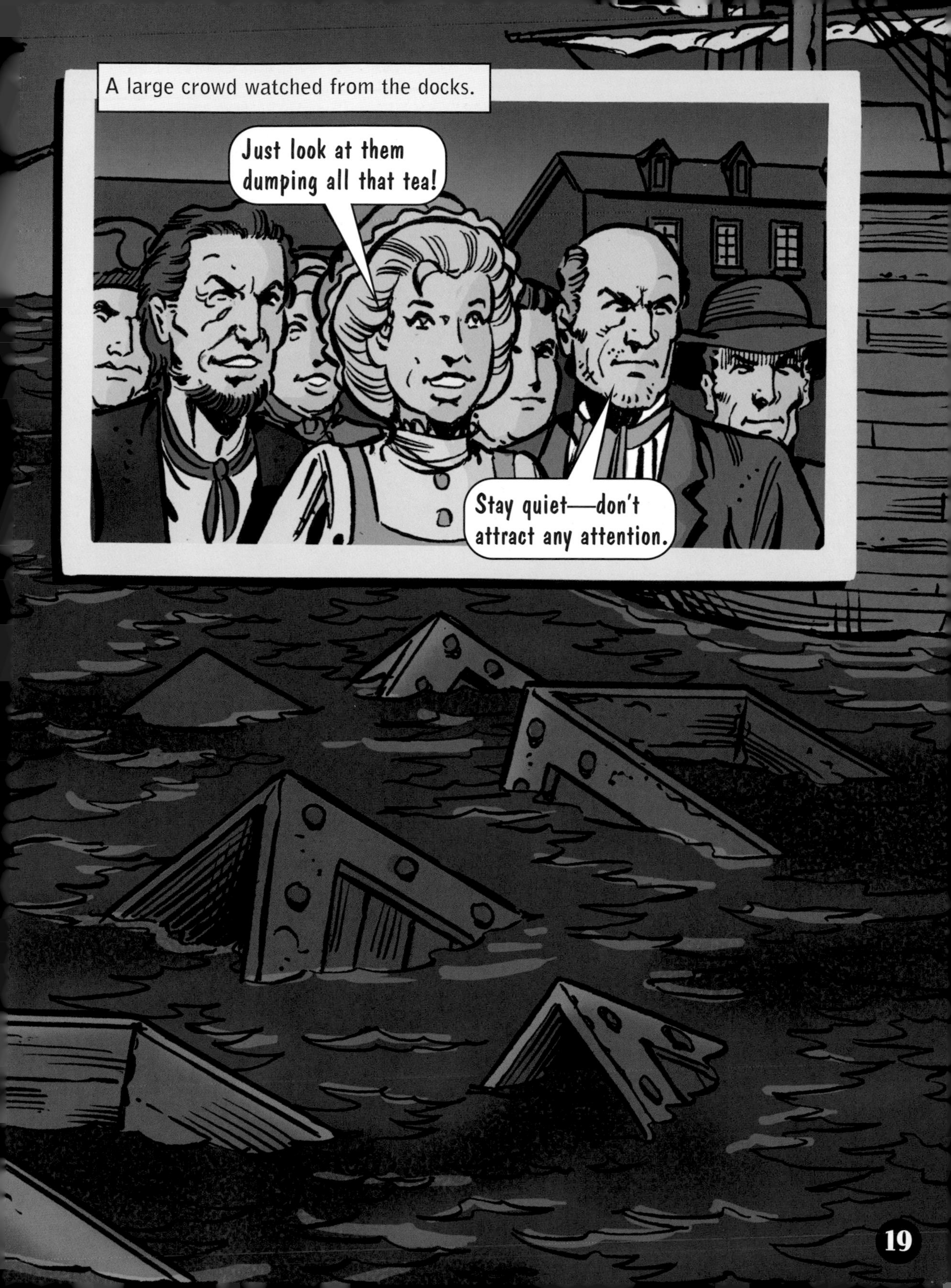
A large crowd watched from the docks.
Just look at them dumping all that tea!
Stay quiet—don't attract any attention.

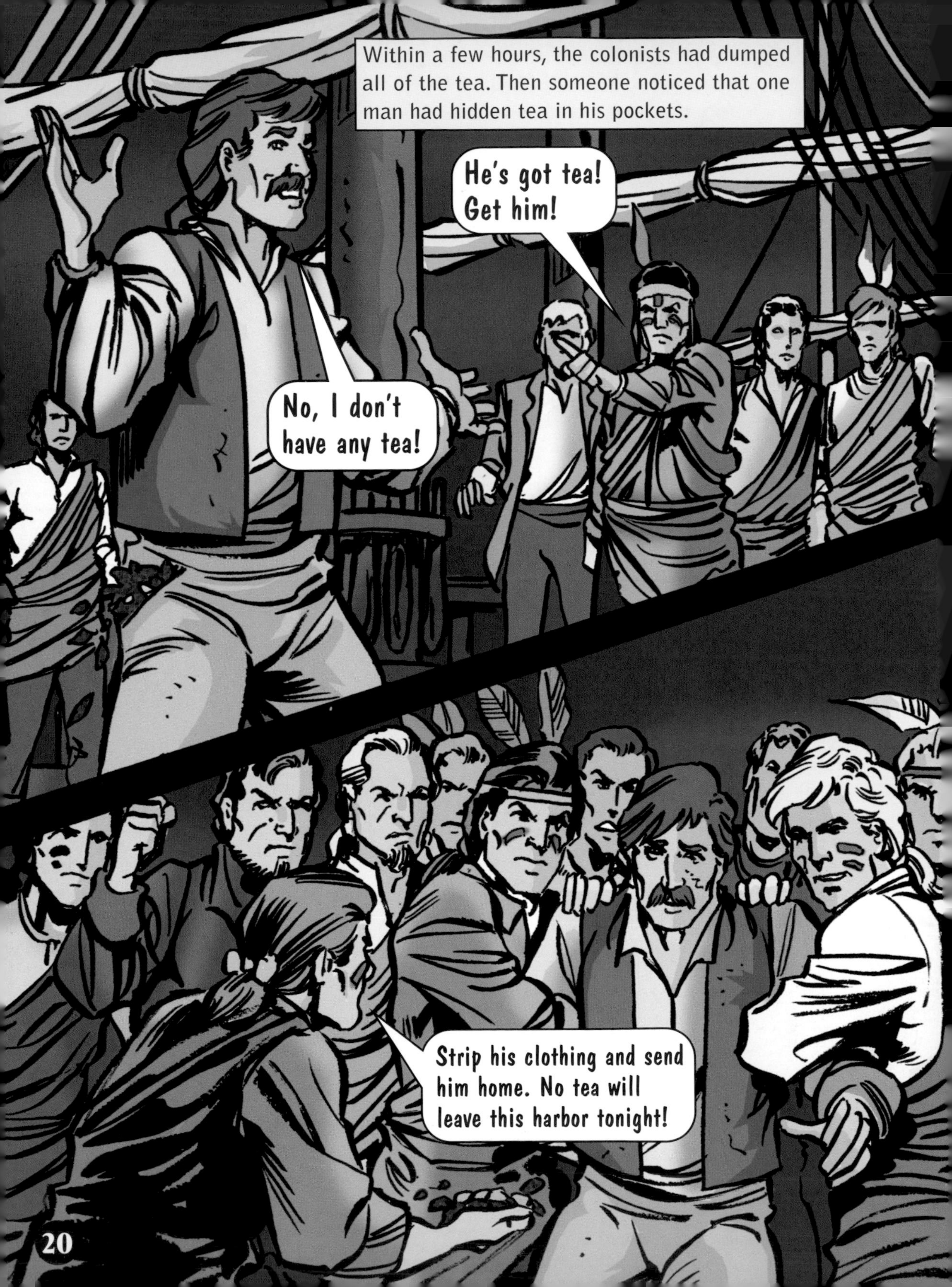
Within a few hours, the colonists had dumped all of the tea. Then someone noticed that one man had hidden tea in his pockets.
He's got tea! Get him!
No, I don't have any tea!
Strip his clothing and send him home. No tea will leave this harbor tonight!

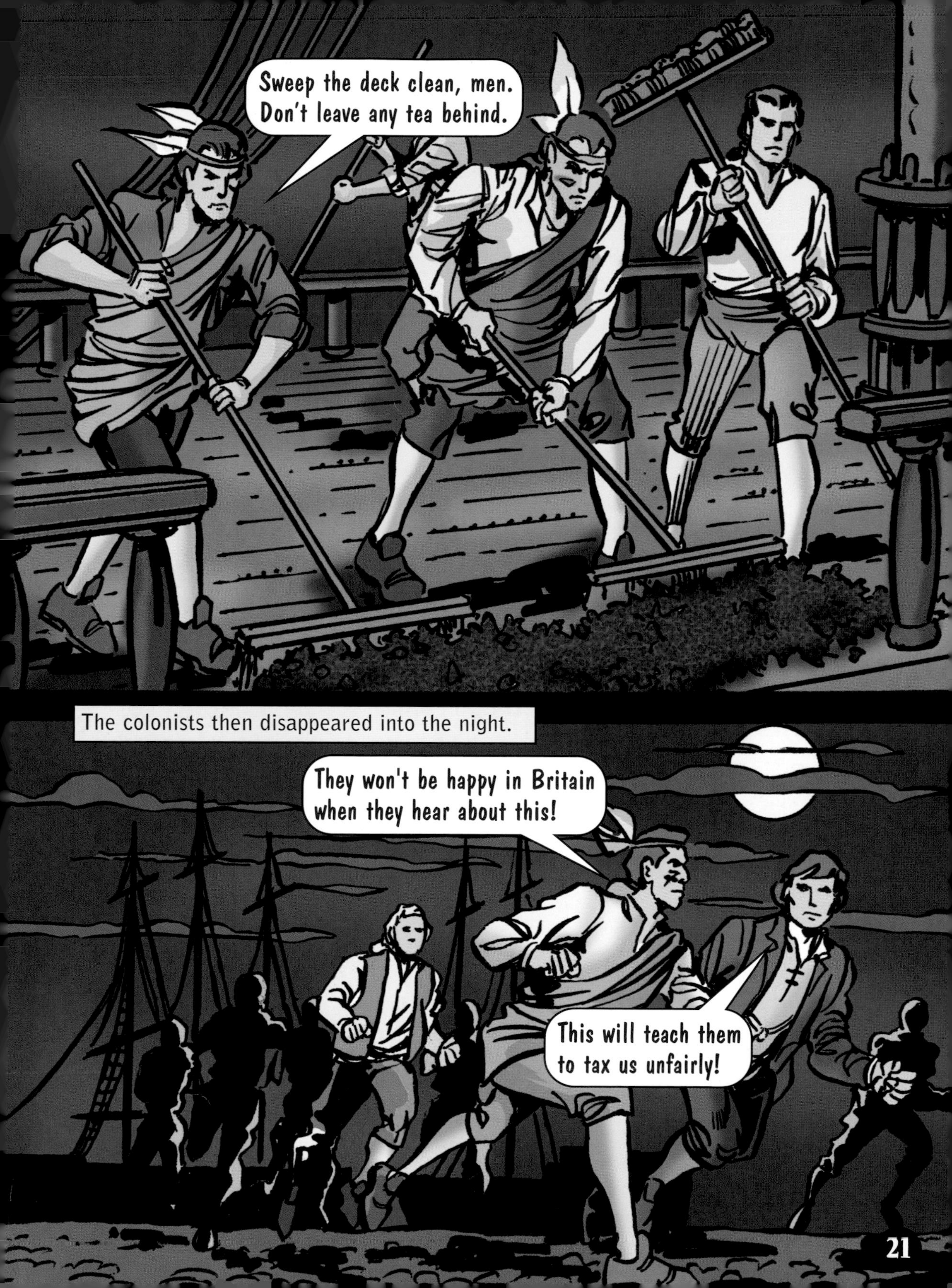

Sweep the deck clean, men. Don't leave any tea behind.
The colonists then disappeared into the night.
They won't be happy in Britain when they hear about this!
This will teach them to tax us unfairly!

# Chapter 4 The Party's Over

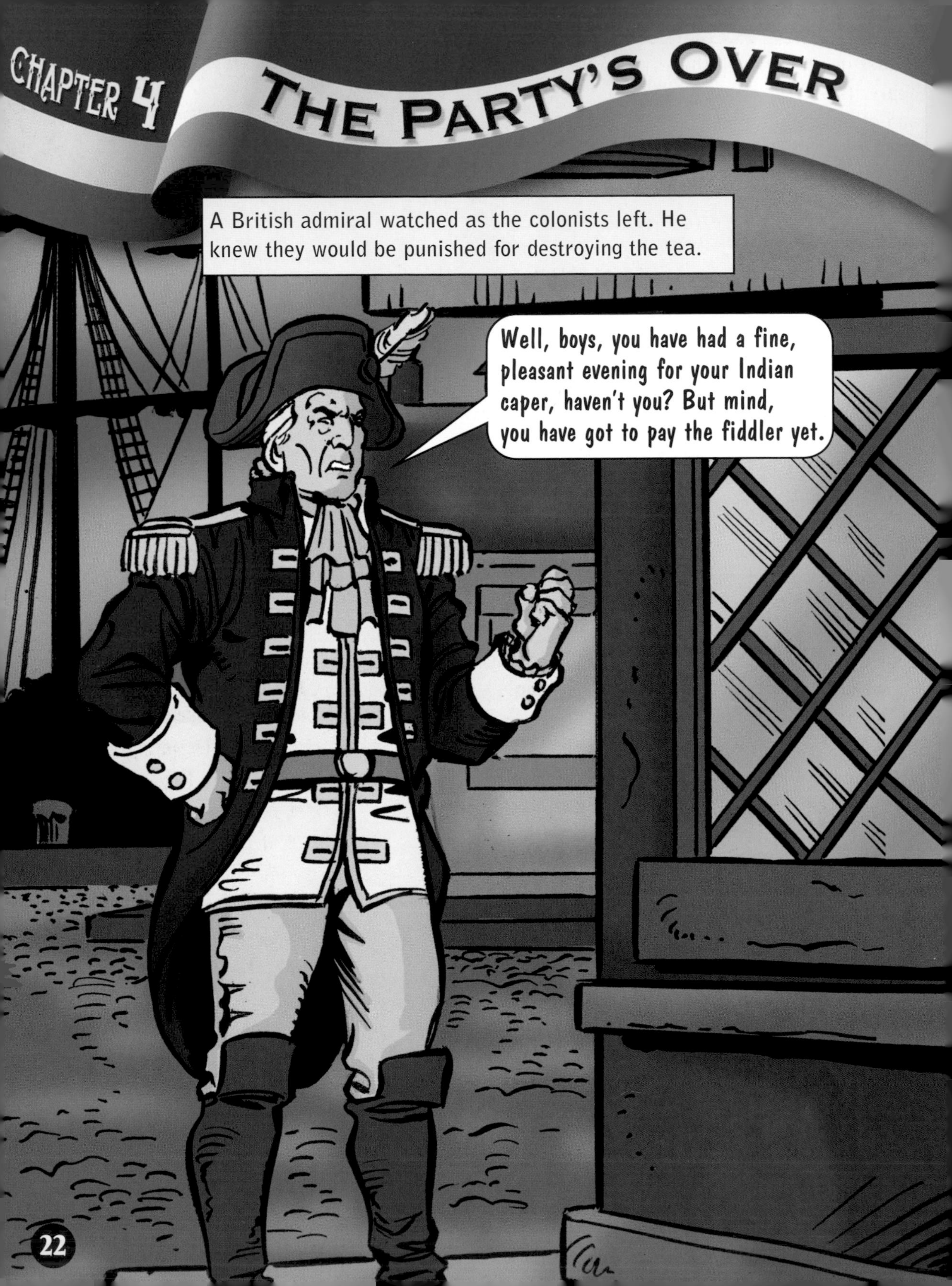
A British admiral watched as the colonists left. He knew they would be punished for destroying the tea.
Well, boys, you have had a fine, pleasant evening for your Indian caper, haven't you? But mind, you have got to pay the fiddler yet.

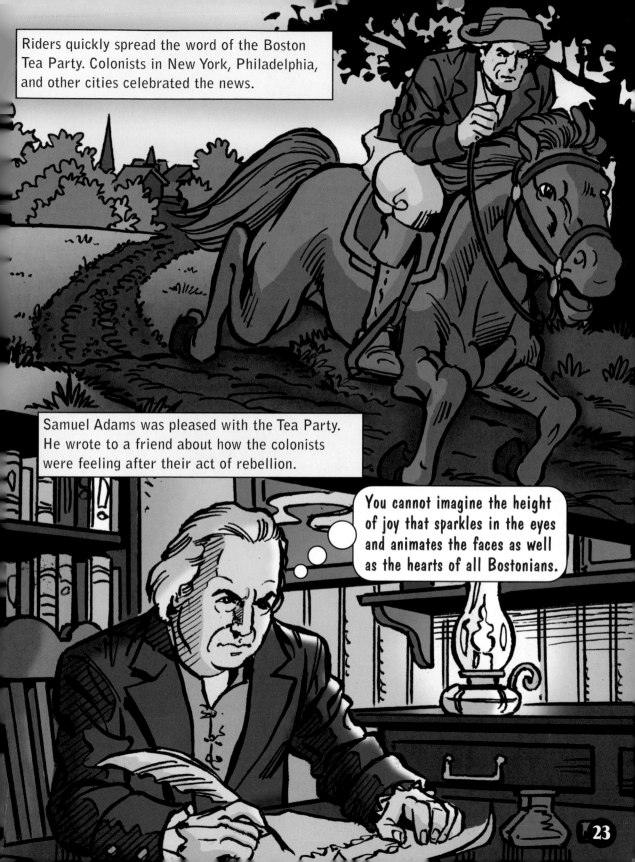

Riders quickly spread the word of the Boston Tea Party. Colonists in New York, Philadelphia, and other cities celebrated the news.

Samuel Adams was pleased with the Tea Party. He wrote to a friend about how the colonists were feeling after their act of rebellion.

You cannot imagine the height of joy that sparkles in the eyes and animates the faces as well as the hearts of all Bostonians.

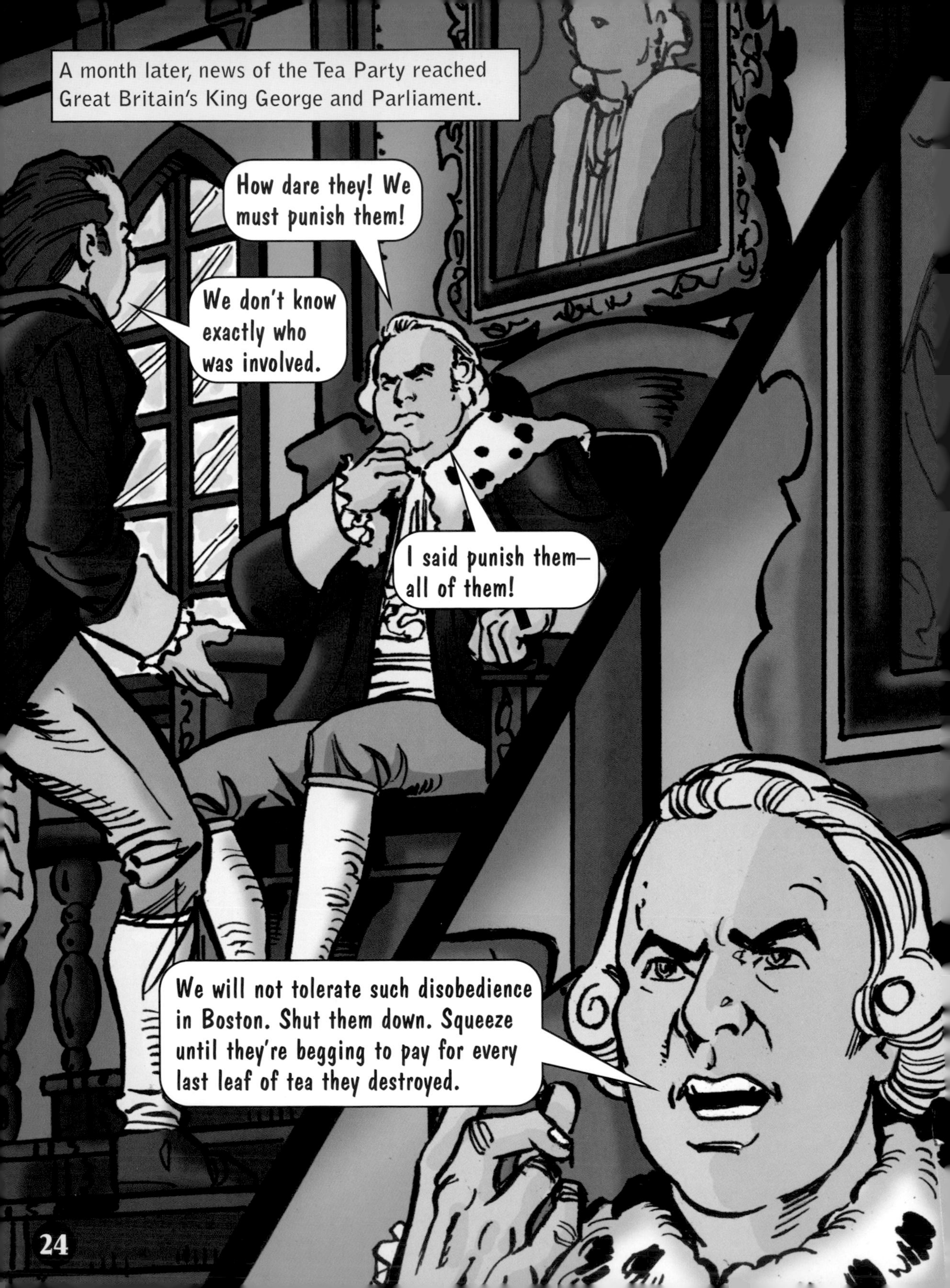
A month later, news of the Tea Party reached Great Britain's King George and Parliament.
How dare they! We must punish them!
We don't know exactly who was involved.
I said punish them—all of them!
We will not tolerate such disobedience in Boston. Shut them down. Squeeze until they're begging to pay for every last leaf of tea they destroyed.

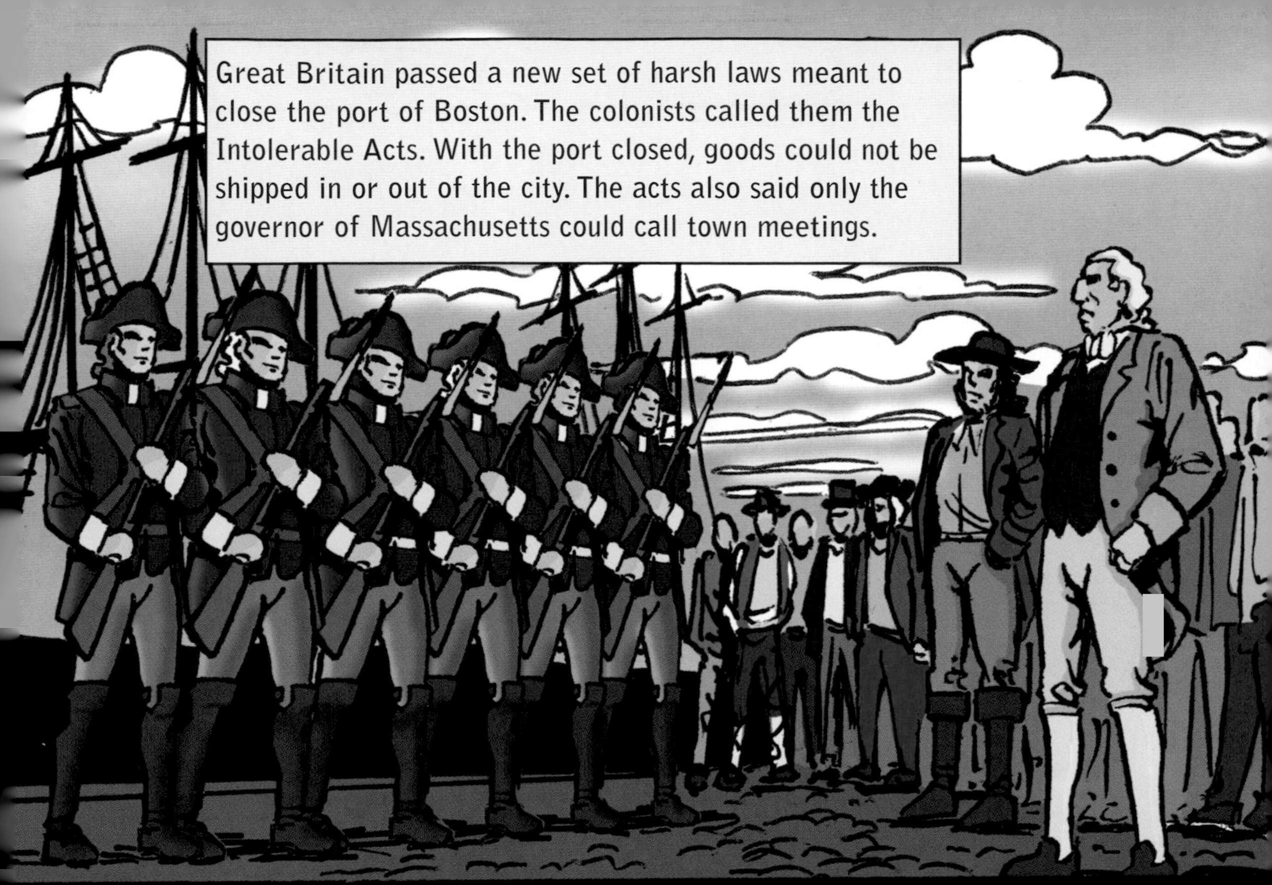
Great Britain passed a new set of harsh laws meant to close the port of Boston. The colonists called them the Intolerable Acts. With the port closed, goods could not be shipped in or out of the city. The acts also said only the governor of Massachusetts could call town meetings.

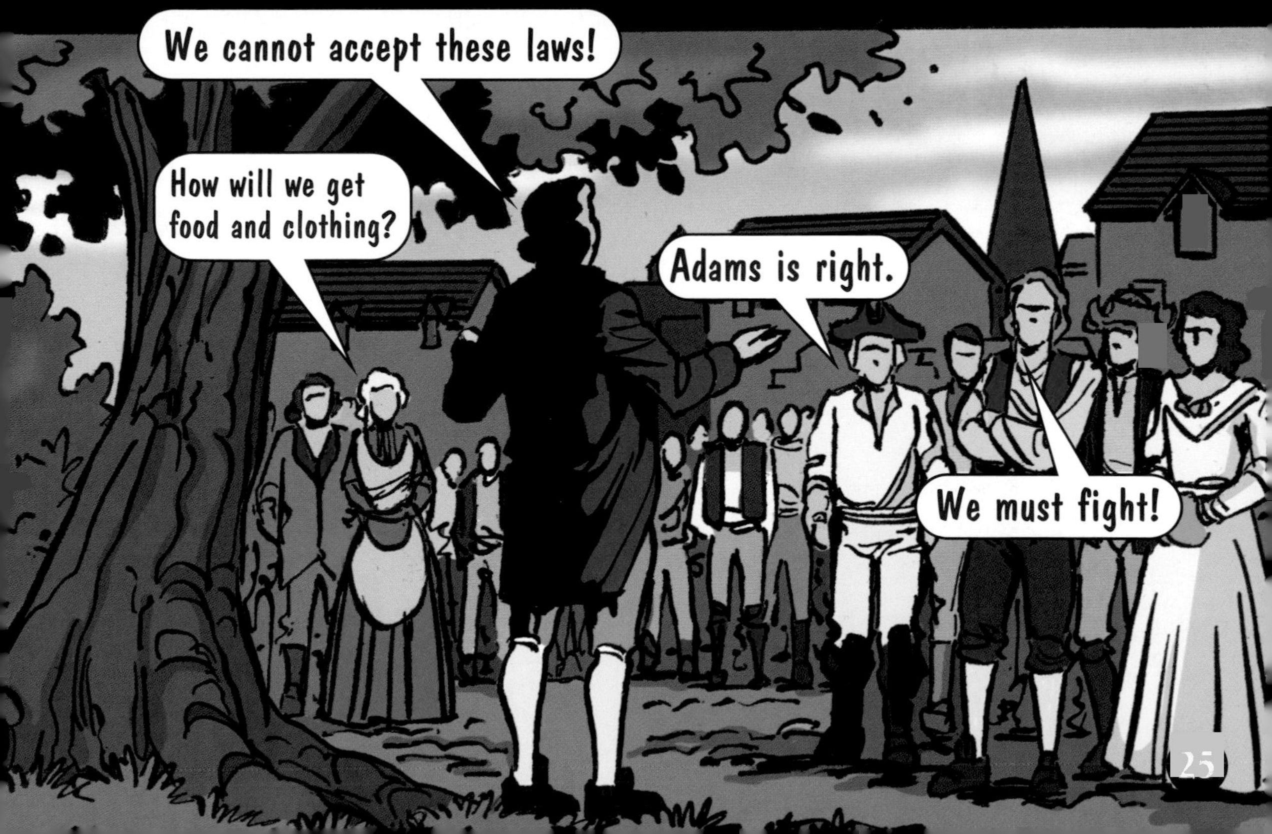
We cannot accept these laws!
How will we get food and clothing?
Adams is right.
We must fight!

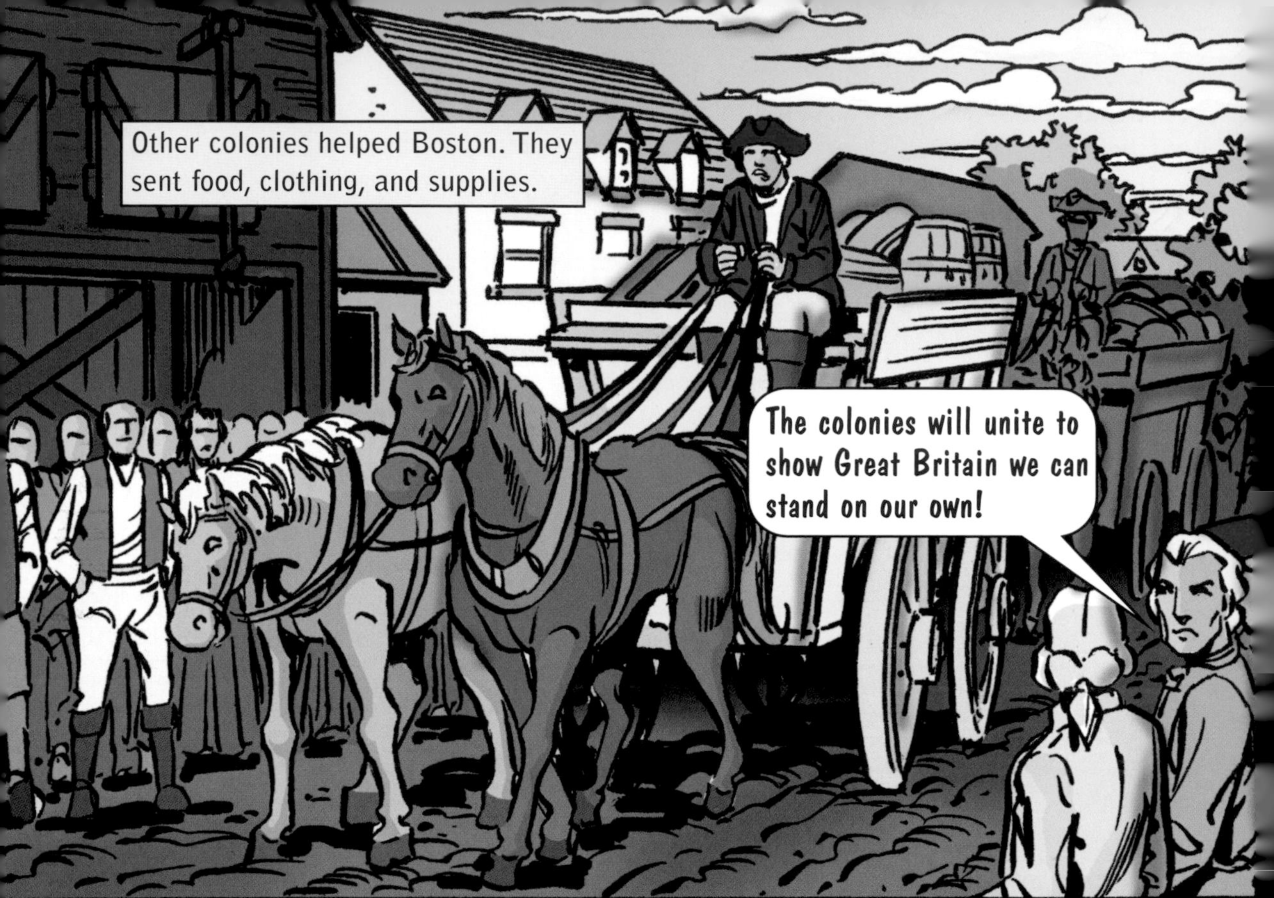
Other colonies helped Boston. They sent food, clothing, and supplies.
The colonies will unite to show Great Britain we can stand on our own!

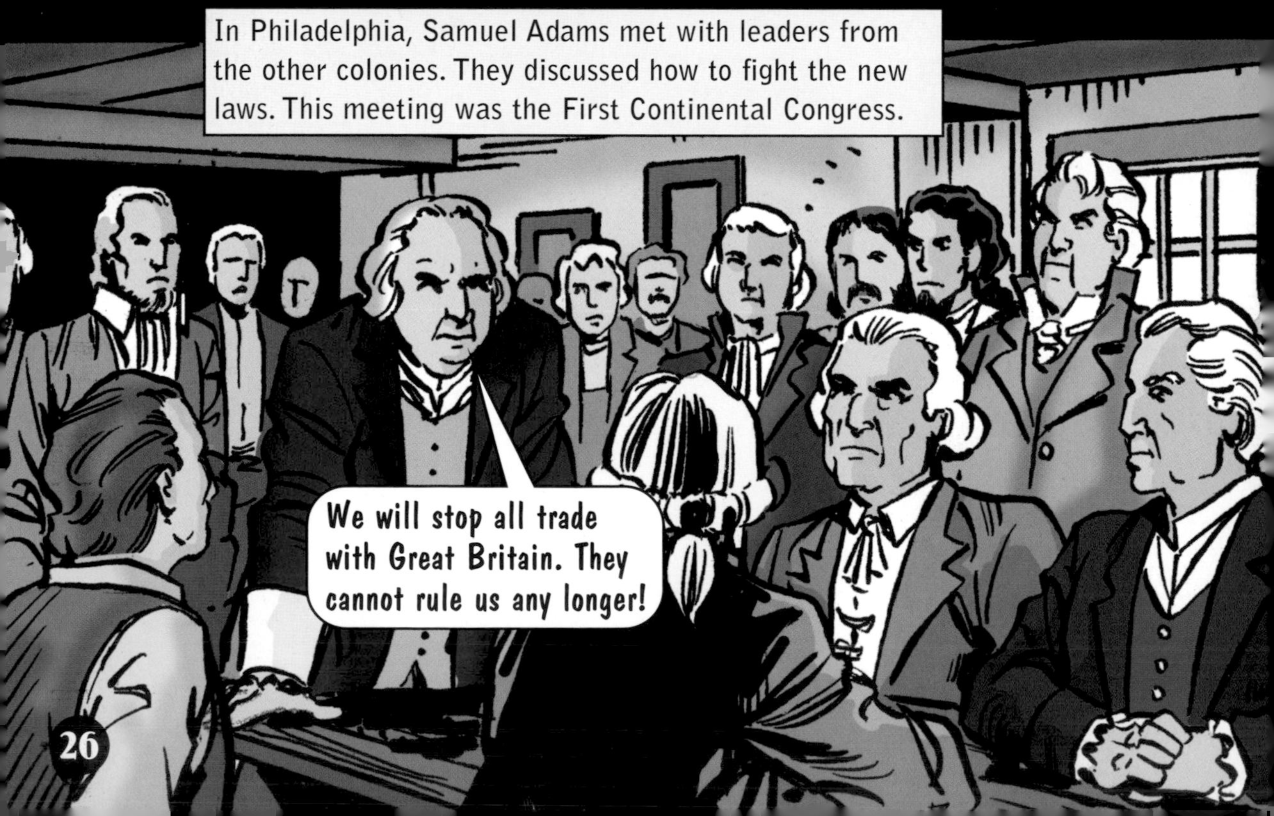
In Philadelphia, Samuel Adams met with leaders from the other colonies. They discussed how to fight the new laws. This meeting was the First Continental Congress.
We will stop all trade with Great Britain. They cannot rule us any longer!

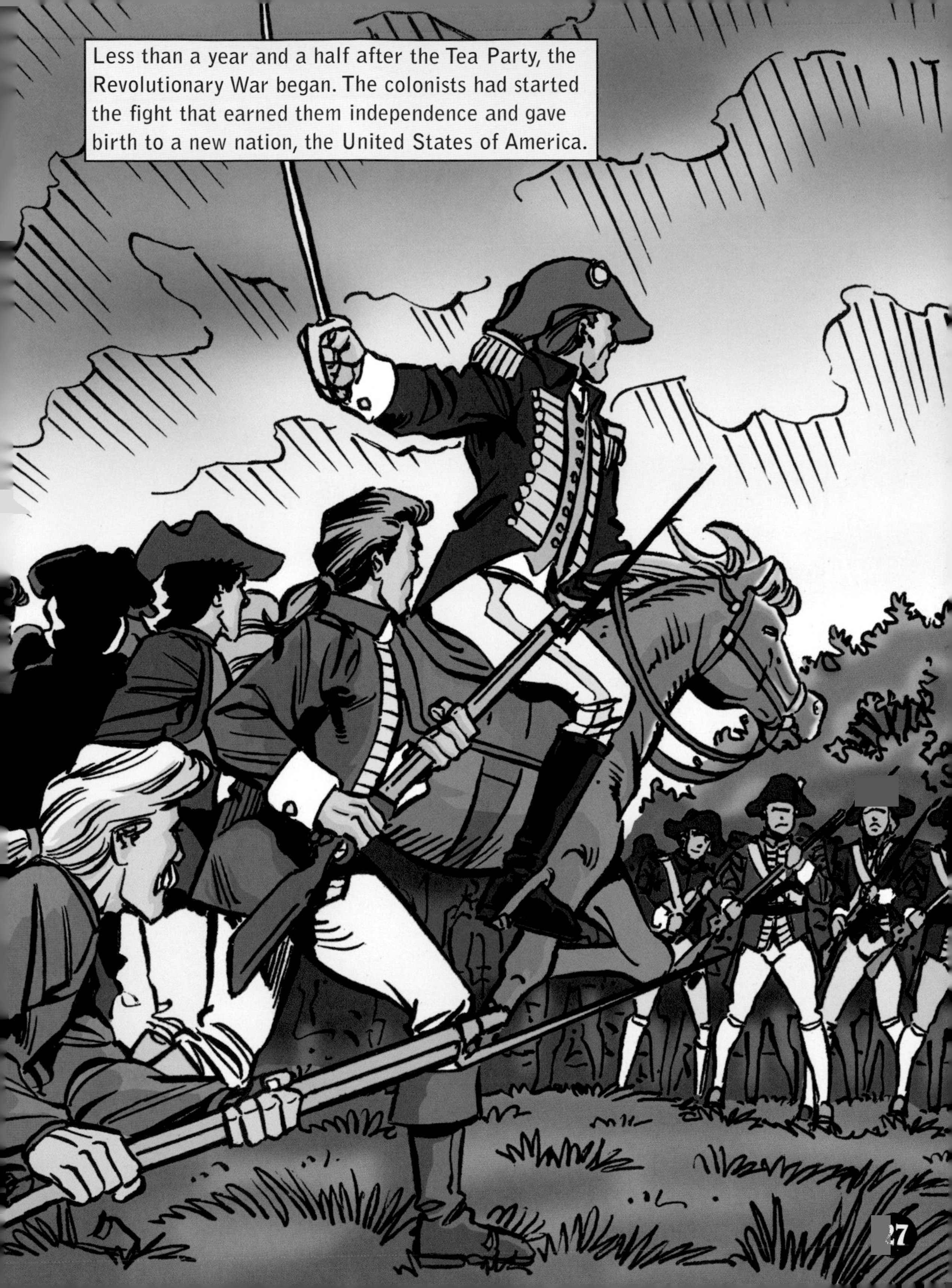
Less than a year and a half after the Tea Party, the Revolutionary War began. The colonists had started the fight that earned them independence and gave birth to a new nation, the United States of America.

# More About The Boston Tea Party

- In 1767, Britain's Parliament passed the Townshend Acts. The acts taxed glass, lead, paint, paper, and tea sold in the colonies. The taxes were supposed to pay the costs of governing the colonies. The taxes angered the colonists because they had no say in how Great Britain ruled them.

- Parliament removed the taxes on all goods except tea in 1770. In 1773, the Tea Act said only the British East India Company could sell taxed tea to the colonists. The Sons of Liberty and other Patriots feared the East India Company would lower the price of tea so much that colonists could not resist buying it, even though it was being taxed. If people bought the taxed tea, Great Britain would keep its control over the colonies.

- In about three hours, the colonists dumped 342 chests, weighing more than 90,000 pounds. The tea they dumped was enough to make about 24 million cups.

Samuel Adams quickly became a major political leader after the Boston Tea Party. He is often called "the father of American independence." Adams was elected governor of Massachusetts in 1794. His cousin John was elected the second president of the United States in 1797.

 In part because of the tea boycott, many colonists became coffee drinkers.

 The Tea Party and other events in Boston, such as the Boston Massacre, were key in starting the movement for independence from Great Britain. Boston is often known as the "cradle of liberty."

# GLOSSARY

**boycott** (BOI-kot)—to refuse to buy certain goods as a means of protest

**caper** (KAY-pur)—a trick or prank

**disobedience** (diss-uh-BEE-dee-uhnss)—going against the rules

**harbor** (HAR-bur)—a place where ships anchor and unload their cargo

**intolerable** (in-TOL-ur-uh-buhl)—unbearable

**Patriot** (PAY-tree-uht)—an American colonist who disagreed with British rule of the colonies

**rebellion** (ri-BEL-yuhn)—a struggle against the people in charge

**taxation** (taks-AY-shuhn)—a requirement that people and businesses pay money to support a government

# INTERNET SITES

FactHound offers a safe, fun way to find Internet sites related to this book. All of the sites on FactHound have been researched by our staff.

Here's how:

1. Visit *www.facthound.com*
2. Type in this special code **0736838465** for age-appropriate sites. Or enter a search word related to this book for a more general search.
3. Click on the **Fetch It** button.

FactHound will fetch the best sites for you!

# Read More

Davis, Kate. *Samuel Adams.* Triangle Histories: Revolutionary War. San Diego, Calif.: Blackbirch Press, 2002.

Dolan, Edward F. *The Boston Tea Party.* Kaleidoscope. New York: Benchmark Books/Marshall Cavendish, 2002.

Furstinger, Nancy. *The Boston Tea Party.* Let Freedom Ring. Mankato, Minn.: Bridgestone Books, 2002.

# Bibliography

Fowler, William M., Jr. *Samuel Adams: Radical Puritan.* New York: Longman, 1997.

Greene, Jack P. *Understanding the American Revolution: Issues and Actors.* Charlottesville: The University Press of Virginia, 1995.

Langguth, A. J. *Patriots.* New York: Simon & Schuster, 1988.

Maier, Pauline. *From Resistance to Revolution: Colonial Radicals and the Development of American Opposition to Britain, 1765–1776.* New York: Alfred A. Knopf, 1972.

Young, Alfred F. *The Shoemaker and the Tea Party: Memory and the American Revolution.* Boston: Beacon Press, 1999.

# INDEX